The Green family has been such an incredible blessing to our nation for such a time as this. *This Dangerous Book* is a must read for all families because it captures the history and impact of the Bible that much of our modern world has forgotten.

—**DAVID AND JASON BENHAM**, entrepreneurs; authors, *Whatever the Cost*

My friends Steve and Jackie Green have written a compelling book that deserves to be read by every person. I highly recommend it.

—**JOHN C. MAXWELL**, bestselling author, speaker, and coach

I love *This Dangerous Book*. It captures the power and essence of the Bible. Read this book!

—**NORM MILLER**, chairman, Interstate Batteries

I am so grateful for the fervor and zeal with which Steve and Jackie Green elevate Scripture, and I trust this resource will help you treasure the gift of God's Word and marvel at his divine means of preserving it throughout time.

—**LOUIE GIGLIO**, pastor, Passion City Church; founder, Passion Conferences

Steve and Jackie Green have managed to write a book filled with all of the history and intrigue that surround this ancient holy text. From the moment I began reading, I simply couldn't put it down.

—**KORIE ROBERTSON**, author, *The Duck Commander Family* and *Strong and Kind*

Many of the most powerful men in history have feared a certain book more than they've feared the most powerful armies and weapons. This book is about that one, and I recommend reading both as soon as possible.

—**ERIC METAXAS**, author, *Bonhoeffer*;
host, *Eric Metaxas Show*

Thanks to Steve and Jackie Green for capturing the incredible history and impact of the Bible. *This Dangerous Book* will stir your soul and help you rediscover the Bible.

—**MARK BATTERSON**, bestselling author;
lead pastor, National Community Church

Extol or excoriate it, the Bible is history's most important book, and here's the powerful story behind its significance and influence. Read it to deepen your understanding and to quicken your heart for God's Word.

—**LEE STROBEL**, author, *The Case for Christ*
and *The Case for Faith*

Even a casual glance at *This Dangerous Book* tells me that Steve and Jackie Green have hit upon a page turner. This book stirs the soul.

—**DR. DAVID JEREMIAH**, senior pastor,
Shadow Mountain Community Church

*This Dangerous Book* will enlighten people of faith and inform the curious. I highly recommend it for anyone who wants to know our history and enjoy even more the truth of Scripture.

—**JAMES LANKFORD**, United States senator

Steve and Jackie Green are doing so much these days to keep God's Scriptures front and center in our world. I have great confidence that reading these pages will increase your love and appreciation for the book that can change your life for eternity.

—**DOUG NUENKE**, US president, The Navigators

I've traveled the world talking to people from all walks of life, and I've always found the Bible to be a point of connection or a point of disagreement or a point of faith. *This Dangerous Book* helps to answer why. I heartily recommend it.

—**GEORGE WOOD**, general superintendent,
Assemblies of God

Steve and Jackie Green have given us a beautiful picture of their personal walk of faith and their founding of the Museum of the Bible in Washington, D.C.

—**STEVE TRICE**, founder and chairman,
Jasco Products Company

As one of the most enduring books in history, the Bible has had quite the journey. Regardless of the reader's religious knowledge or beliefs, I know they'll be intrigued as they learn more about the Bible's influence on our culture.

—**BOBBY GRUENEWALD**, innovation pastor, Life.Church;
founder, YouVersion Bible App

*This Dangerous Book* has earned my highest recommendation. It is a must read for any Christian or any curious person.

—**ROY L. PETERSON**, president and CEO,
American Bible Society

*This Dangerous Book*, like the Bible and the Museum of the Bible that it chronicles, presents a "cabinet of wonder" that the inquisitive, be they a student or a skeptic of Scripture, will find accessible and relevant.

—**CURTIS V. HAIL**, chairman emeritus,
e3 Partners/I Am Second

Steve and Jackie Green are truly people of the Book. Read along as the Greens guide you through the story of the Bible and the museum that bears its name.

—**RUSSELL MOORE**, president, The Ethics and Religious Liberty Commission of the Southern Baptist Convention

In *This Dangerous Book*, Steve and Jackie Green tell the compelling story of the one source of truth feared more than any other. Everyone needs to read this book.

—**DAVID BARTON**, author; historian; founder and president, WallBuilders

We all need to be powerfully reminded of where we came from and where we fit in a larger context in relationship to the Bible. *This Dangerous Book* does just that.

—**ROB HOSKINS**, president, OneHope, Inc.

# THIS
# DANGEROUS
# BOOK

# THIS DANGEROUS BOOK

### HOW THE **BIBLE** HAS SHAPED OUR WORLD
### AND WHY IT STILL MATTERS TODAY

## STEVE AND JACKIE GREEN

### WITH BILL HIGH

ZONDERVAN
BOOKS

ZONDERVAN BOOKS

*This Dangerous Book*
Copyright © 2017 by Steve Green, Jackie Green, and William High

Requests for information should be addressed to:
Zondervan, *3900 Sparks Dr. SE, Grand Rapids, Michigan 49546*

Zondervan titles may be purchased in bulk for educational, business, fundraising, or sales promotional use. For information, please email SpecialMarkets@Zondervan.com.

ISBN 978-0-310-36704-8 (softcover)
ISBN 978-0-310-35152-8 (audio)
ISBN 978-0-310-35148-1 (ebook)

Library of Congress Cataloging-in-Publication Data

Names: Green, Steve, 1963- author. | Green, Jackie, 1965- author. | High, Bill, author.
Title: This dangerous book : how the Bible has shaped our world and why it still matters today
/ Steve and Jackie Green, with Bill High.
Description: Grand Rapids, Michigan : Zondervan, [2017] | Includes bibliographical
references and index.
Identifiers: LCCN 2017039487 | ISBN 9780310351474 (hardcover)
Subjects: LCSH: Bible—History. | Bible—Introductions. | Museum of the Bible.
Classification: LCC BS445 .G74 2017 | DDC 220—dc23 LC record available at https://lccn
.loc.gov/2017039487

Authors are represented by The Christopher Ferebee Agency, www.christopherferebee.com.

*Cover design: Faceout Studio*
*Interior design: Kait Lamphere*
*Interior photography management: Kim Tanner, Chelcie Hunt*

*Printed in the United States of America*

HB 01.07.2025

*Dedicated to the many who have gone before us*
*translating, copying, and transmitting the Scriptures*
*so that we might have the Bible today*

# CONTENTS

## PART 4: APPEAL TO HEAVEN

## PART 5: TO THE ENDS OF THE EARTH

# FOREWORD

This book is the captivating story of a normal family who decided, as much as possible, to build their lives, their family, and their family business on the Bible, God's Word, and what happened as a result. Their amazing adventures, moving miracles, and bountiful blessings are all testimonies of God's faithfulness to those who commit to following his instructions.

Throughout the Bible, God repeatedly promises all kinds of blessings to anyone who will honor and treasure his Word, read and study his Word, and remember and meditate on his Word. But most important of all, God promises to bless those who trust and obey his Word.

Consider just four of God's promises:

1. "Always remember what is written in the Book of God's Law. Think about it day and night to be sure that you always obey everything written in it. If you consistently do this, you will prosper and be successful" (Josh. 1:8).
2. "Blessed is the man who does not follow the advice of the wicked . . . but instead, he delights in Word of the Lord, and he meditates on it day and night. That man will be like a tree growing by a riverbank—he will produce consistent

fruit each season, his leaves will never wither, and whatever he does will prosper" (Ps. 1:1–3).

3. "Anyone who listens and trust my words, and puts them into practice is like a wise man who built his house on solid rock. The rain came down, the streams rose, and the winds beat against that house; yet it did not fall apart, because its foundation was rock solid. But everyone who ignores my Word and does not put it into practice is like a foolish man who built his house on unstable sand" (Matt. 7:24–26).

4. "If you keep looking steadily into God's perfect Word which gives you freedom, and you continue to do this, not forgetting what you learn, but instead practicing all that it tells you to do, then you will be blessed in everything you do!" (James 1:25).

As you will learn in reading this book, the lives of Steve and Jackie Green, along with their parents and their children, are dramatic proof that God keeps his promises.

For two thousand years, the Bible has been both the bestselling book and the most translated book in the world, year after year after year. No other book comes close to the Bible's impact and influence in transforming individuals, strengthening families, shaping nations, and determining human history. But just because someone owns a Bible does not guarantee that they will be transformed by it. That Bible must be opened and read and obeyed.

Today, there are more Bibles in print than ever before, but a Bible on the shelf is worthless. Millions of people are plagued with spiritual anorexia, starving to death from spiritual malnutrition, because they ignore the Bible. Just as you cannot be physically healthy without eating nutritious food every day, you cannot be spiritually healthy without feeding daily on God's Word. Jesus said, "People cannot live by eating only bread; they must feed on every word of God" (Matt. 4:4).

It is my prayer that *this* book will make you hungry to know *the* book!

As you learn of Steve and Jackie's journey of faith, and as you see how God's Word has guided, comforted, challenged, and sustained them through all the ups and downs of life, I hope you will commit the rest of your life to three activities:

1. Accepting the authority of God's Word over my life
2. Assimilating the truths of God's Word in my life
3. Applying the principles of God's Word to my life

If you want to become all that God has designed you to be, you must build your life on the Bible. The Spirit of God uses the Word of God to make us like the Son of God.

I'd love to hear your story of how this book leads you to the Book. If you write to me (Rick@DailyHope.com), I will pray for you in your journey, just as I have for my dear friends Steve and Jackie. May God bless you!

—Rick Warren, author, *The Purpose Driven Life*; teacher, Daily Hope Radio and Podcast

# ACKNOWLEDGMENTS

We began this writing journey in a year with our calendars already full. It has been a crazy and busy venture that would not have been possible without the support, encouragement, understanding, and selflessness of others.

Derek and Erica, Lauren and Michael, Lindy, Danielle and Caleb, Grace, and Gabi: we have been blessed more than we ever imagined with a house full of wonderful kids! You make us proud.

Mary-Kate, Fenix, Cruz, and Luca: it is so much fun being your GiGi and Poppy!

Tim Willard: we are so grateful for the countless hours you spent working with us to make the manuscript just right. You did a great job of keeping things lighthearted, and we appreciated your quick wit.

Many thanks to the administrative team at Hobby Lobby Corporate. Marsha Bold: you worked tirelessly to keep up with our complicated schedules and get us where we needed to be, always having a joyful spirit about you. Pam Lunsford and Janice Roberts: you two round out the team with your talents and abilities. We appreciate you more than you know.

Joshua Charles: your last-minute contributions were right on time for rounding out our manuscript.

Our agent, Chris Ferebee: we greatly appreciate your getting us to this occasion.

Our friends Jim and Cecelia: thanks for letting us enjoy your home in a setting full of God's grandeur as we began writing.

Bill High: we are grateful for your encouragement to begin this journey and the assistance to make it happen. Thanks for believing in us!

Zondervan team: you were a delight to work with!

Museum of the Bible staff: what a joy it is to know so many wonderful, gifted, serving, hardworking people who have worked diligently to make a dream come true.

Our family: we love you all and feel incredibly blessed to have you in our lives. Thank you for understanding and allowing us to take the time necessary to accomplish this goal.

Our parents, David and Barbara and Jack and Nita: we have both been blessed beyond measure to have parents who gave us through their words and deeds an appreciation and love for God's Word. We are proud to call you our parents and will forever be grateful.

# INTRODUCTION

The Bible.

When you hear those two words, what do they make you think of? For thousands of years, those two words have sparked a variety of emotions. Those emotions range from deep devotion to downright hatred. And of course, there's an entire middle ground of apathy—just another book.

Indeed, the Bible has stirred up controversies that have affected empires. People have been burned alive in their attempt to translate it for the common person. Nations have misused its contents to justify bad behavior. It's been used against science and leveraged for political gain.

But it's also been the source behind those who worked in England to abolish the slave trade. It has been the source for leaders like Martin Luther King Jr., Mother Teresa, and John Adams. It has changed cultural views on women, children, and the oppressed. It guided the first Christians in the first century toward a morality unseen in the Roman world. It moved a young monk to call out injustices in the church, an act which led to the Protestant Reformation.

It has inspired artists such as Bach and Rembrandt. It was the guiding light for world-changing intellectuals like Blaise Pascal. Its printing was one of the most significant events of the last millennia.

15

The discovery of the Dead Sea Scrolls is one of the most important archaeological discoveries of the twentieth century.

The Bible is a wonderful, dangerous book. It's an interesting, polarizing, confusing, and beautiful book. Hollywood makes movies about its characters. One of the most popular movies of all time is Mel Gibson's *The Passion*. And who can forget Charlton Heston as Moses in *The Ten Commandments*? Okay, that might be dating us a bit, but we recommend you check it out if you haven't seen it.

The Bible lives in our nation's cultural fabric. It continues to influence people and nations the world over.

Should we ignore it?

Dismiss it?

That's why we are writing this book. We believe that the Bible deserves our attention and study. Whether you are a believer or an opponent, you ought to know what this book is about. Even the most ardent critics have argued that the study of the Bible is essential to understanding our world.

This book reflects our own journey while at the same time reflecting a broader journey of so many people. We grew up in Oklahoma, in Christian families who actively served in their churches. As children and teenagers, we went to Christian camps and youth conferences. Actually, the first time we met was at a church camp, although we didn't start dating until later.

We dated just like normal people. Fell in love just like normal people. Got married, bought a house, and started a family just like so many people do in this country. We both worked for the family business. Our parents taught us to work hard, live with integrity, and give at least a tenth of our resources to God as a way to worship him.

Like so many young families, we had to wrestle with raising children, making ends meet financially, dealing with debt, and budgeting. In our case, we looked to the Bible for answers. We believe, like billions of people in the world, that the Bible is what it claims to be, the inspired word of God. That doesn't mean God wrote down his thoughts and sent them to us thousands of years ago. Rather, it means that God was guiding the writers of the Bible. We believe God speaks to us today through those writings.

We read the Bible as a source of devotion for our faith. We, as a couple and family, spend time in it regularly. In times of hardship, we go to the Bible. In times of worship and joy, we go to the Bible. The great Christian evangelist Billy Graham said, "The Christian life is not a constant high. I have my moments of deep discouragement. I have to go to God in prayer with tears in my eyes, and say, 'O God, forgive me,' or 'Help me.'" We've been there.

The Christian faith is not about being perfect and never making mistakes. It's about doing our best to follow Jesus Christ. We do our best. But we're not perfect. We stumble and fall. That's what the Christian faith is all about: second chances, forgiveness, and grace. And it's available to anyone who desires it.

In 2009, our lives began to change dramatically. That's when we first bought a biblical manuscript. At the time, we had no idea what that would lead to. You'll read more about that winding road in the coming pages. It's been an exciting, challenging, and invigorating adventure to establish the United States' first Museum of the Bible in Washington, D.C.

Some people have questioned our motives. They've scoffed, "A Christian family establishing a museum of the Bible!" (As a side note, it's hard to imagine an atheist wanting to establish a Bible museum.) Belief in something does not disqualify a person from speaking out in favor of it. If that were true, millions of Americans would be disqualified from speaking out for the principles found in the Declaration of Independence. Believing "all men are created equal" does not disqualify you from celebrating that "all men are created equal."

There's no doubt that every person brings some kind of belief with them to any discussion, argument, debate, or research. But that personal belief does not disqualify their participation. We can be reasonable people, aware of our beliefs toward a certain worldview. We can then acknowledge that, set those beliefs aside, and still carry on an intelligent and fair discussion of the facts.

For instance, as the Museum of the Bible project first came to life, we knew and understood that we would need a museum that all people could visit. We would not promote our faith but could present the facts. We've sought out the best scholars from all around the world to be part of the efforts, including those with differing viewpoints. The experience for anyone attending should be educational, interesting, and inviting.

We knew we would receive criticism from both sides of the aisle. Some have argued we are simply trying to proselytize, while others have advocated that we need to take a more evangelistic viewpoint in the museum. Yet throughout the process, we've continued to pursue a factual presentation of the Bible.

We know that we won't satisfy everyone. There will still be critics who will challenge our methods and motives. At the end of the day, that's okay, as long as those same people will be willing to engage in an honest look at the Bible. Like it or not, the Bible simply cannot be ignored.

Our story is your story; it's the nation's story. We've found what men like George Washington and John Adams discovered: the Bible is more than an ancient artifact; its voice possesses the power to shape the world for good. Our sincere hope is that you will be encouraged and intrigued by this book. We hope you'll visit the museum with your friends or family and take it in, ask questions, and press into this book called the Bible.

We think one of the most beautiful aspects of the Bible is that it invites *all*. In the Old Testament book of Psalms, David wrote a poem in which he invites readers to experience God for themselves: "Taste and see that the LORD is good; blessed is the one who takes refuge in him. . . . The lions may grow weak and hungry, but those who seek the LORD lack no good thing" (Ps. 34:8, 10).

David essentially says, "Come and see for yourself. Try it out!"

We ask you to join us as we unfold this little story about something important and intriguing to us: the Bible. We'll pepper in our own story and give you a peek at our own journey as a couple seeking to follow the principles of the Bible.

But more than our story, we want to give you a glimpse of some of the things we've learned from this wonderful, dangerous book.

# PART 1

# THE STORY BEGINS

שְׁמַע יִשְׂרָאֵל

*Hear, O Israel: The LORD our God, the LORD is one.*
—DEUTERONOMY 6:4

*The Bible assumes as a self-evident fact that men can know God with at least the same degree of immediacy as they know any other person or thing that comes within the field of their experience.*
—A. W. TOZER, *THE PURSUIT OF GOD*

CHAPTER 1

# ON A PLANE TO
# A HOLY GRAIL

*England has two books, the Bible and Shakespeare. England made
Shakespeare, but the Bible made England.*

—VICTOR HUGO

*The word of God is living and active, sharper than any two-edged
sword, piercing to the division of soul and of spirit, of joints and of
marrow, and discerning the thoughts and intentions of the heart.*

—HEBREWS 4:12 ESV

*After supper she got out her book and learned me about Moses and
the Bulrushers; and I was in a sweat to find out all about him;
but by-and-by she let out Moses had been dead a considerable long
time; so then I didn't care no more about him; because I don't take
no stock in dead people.*

—HUCKLEBERRY FINN

**H**ow did we get to this point?

Sitting on a plane headed to Turkey, you tend to ask yourself questions like this. Weeks earlier, some acquaintances had asked for help. We were business people—with ancient Bibles, to be more specific. The idea was to collect historical Bibles with the hopes of one day opening a museum for the Bible in Dallas, Texas.

"There's a great opportunity to acquire a very old manuscript of the gospel of John written on purple vellum with gold lettering," they said. "A family owns it and is motivated to sell it."

The family sent us a little homemade video of the manuscript. They kept it in an ornate silver case. It was precious to them.

"Perhaps you can go with us to Turkey and have a look at it. While we are overseas, we can arrange to meet with other contacts we have as well."

We live in the business world. So it's easy for us to approach opportunities through that lens. And that's what we did here. Our family has had a love for the Bible, so there was a natural interest in the idea of celebrating it. We liked the idea of a museum for the Bible, and we certainly liked the thought of helping folks acquire a collection of Bibles, and rather more important, Bibles of historical and religious value.

We thought about the opportunity as a family and decided to go for it. So I left with our acquaintances in November of 2009. The family who owned the artifact had asked if we'd meet them in their hometown.

"We'll meet you in Istanbul," we said. So we flew out to Istanbul.

The family lived in a very unstable rural area where just a few weeks earlier, two Baptist missionaries were killed during their travels. We decided not to go to their hometown. It was too dangerous. And they did not make the trip to meet us in Istanbul. In the end, the family decided not to sell the manuscript, and therefore we never acquired it. Unbeknownst to me, the trip to Istanbul was only the beginning of this new adventure.

On this first trip, our contacts took me to Israel as well to meet with several dealers in the world of Bible collecting. We attended several meetings, with people in Turkey and Israel, about Bible-related collections that might be available for sale. Even though we made the trip to inquire about the gospel of John artifact in Istanbul, I began to get excited about the mounting opportunities to put together a more extensive Bible collection that could become a central feature of a museum for people around the world to visit.

I remember while in Istanbul going to a museum exhibit and wondering about some of the items that were being displayed. They claimed that one piece of wood was part of the cross that Jesus died on. The chances of that were slim to none, and it was an indication of the challenges we would face in this world.

Because of people's passion for this book, many folks are willing to believe anything, desperately wanting to prove what they believe to be true. As with any valuable collectible, there are always con artists trying to take advantage of those who are passionate about collecting those items. Even as we were touring Jerusalem, it was pointed out that many of the "Holy" sites may not be the actual site they claim to be. In Jerusalem, for example, there are very few places that could be the actual spot where Jesus walked. Many of the streets from the first century are several feet under the current roads of Old Jerusalem. The desire to connect with a person's faith is real and powerful. That passion, as with any passion, can be preyed upon.

The market for forgeries is real, and it is one of the dangers in this world of collecting artifacts. All museums have them. The forgers become more sophisticated, as does the equipment to detect their forgeries.

I returned to Oklahoma City, and life went back to normal. Over the next several months, we were kept informed on new opportunities to purchase historical Bibles and manuscripts. As purchase opportunities arose, we would consider a buy. The passion for these items lit up in us like a spark beneath dry wood. It's only a matter of time before the fire rages.

The trip to Turkey and Israel was eye-opening. To see firsthand many biblical artifacts! This was a whole new world we knew nothing about but were excited to explore. Little did we know we'd embarked upon an adventure that would prove to have meaning for us as a family, for our nation, and for the world.

## A History of Adventure

In the latter part of the nineteenth century, the new wave of scientists, fueled mostly by the influential thought of Charles Darwin, was on the rise. It was a time of change. New scientific ideas captured the minds of the world. Scientists and academics, in many cases, ascended above the theologian and the minister. The once-dominant religious thinkers were now being supplanted by scientists who pushed a skepticism about the Bible that said if the world and its species were subject to long processes of development, then why not the Bible.

This thinking caused a stir among many in religious circles and, in particular, at Cambridge University, where some took these new ideas to heart and searched hard for evidence that would help support earlier dates for the original manuscript writing of the New Testament.

So just prior to the twentieth century, biblical artifacts were a hot commodity. Not simply for posterity but as evidence to prove the veracity of the Bible.

It was during this age of skepticism and heightened desire for discovering new biblical artifacts that Scottish twin sisters Agnes and Margaret Smith made a stunning discovery.

The sisters were an interesting pair. They were left without their mother; she died when they were infants. They enjoyed a deep and loving relationship with their father, who vowed never to marry again after losing his wife. He'd bring the girls up on his own. They received an incredible education, mostly from their father in Scotland, an education balanced by travel and play.

Their father had made a deal with them. If they learned a language, he would take them on a trip to that country. The incentive worked. The young girls excelled in languages, mastering French, German, Spanish, and Italian. They grew to possess a deep desire to travel—an adventurous spirit inherited from their father and spurred on by their grasp of languages.

After their beloved father passed away, they lived alone in a massive home in Cambridge called Castle Hill and engaged in eccentricities like exercising in their garden with parallel bars. Their inheritance was contingent upon their father's request that they never live apart.

Not long after their father died, the older sister, Margaret, married fifty-seven-year-old James Gibson. The six-month honeymoon was the longest the sisters had ever been separated. But their marriage did not endure. James died only three years later, in October of 1886.

Margaret's sister, Agnes, did not fare much better. She married Samuel Lewis, Fellow of Corpus Christi College, Cambridge, who endured the unfortunate nickname "Satan" Lewis. Apparently, Samuel, peering down from his window at the college, noticed a wedding taking place. When the bride looked up and saw the "notoriously ugly man with a straggling black beard peering down into the gloom of the Church from above, she cried 'Satan!' and fainted."[1]

Agnes was married just over three years when she joined her sister as a widow. She and Samuel were in Oxford, heading back home to Cambridge. They had to wait forty minutes for their train, so Agnes waited for Samuel in the tearoom of the station while Samuel ran a quick errand. When he returned, he hopped on the train with Agnes, sat down next to her, "commented on an illustration in the Arabic newspaper she was reading then fell back with a sigh and was dead."[2]

Alone once again, the sisters made a life for themselves in Cambridge, but they were not the sort of ladies you might think suited for nine-day caravans across the deserts of the Sinai Peninsula, an area where just a decade earlier, a Cambridge professor had been murdered by bandits. They held no educational pedigree—let alone a university degree!—except that they were both gifted in languages with an obvious desire to expand their knowledge.

Years earlier, in 1885, the sisters had desired to travel to Sinai, but Margaret's husband deterred them. Now they found themselves in the curious position in which nothing was preventing them from taking on such an adventure, dangerous as it was.

And so they embarked on a journey to faraway lands, in an intense search for ancient biblical manuscripts—and found them![3] On their trip to the Sinai Peninsula, they visited Saint Catherine's Monastery at Mount Sinai. One of the manuscripts they found contained the largest portion of Scripture in Aramaic! This was the language that Jesus probably spoke in his home.

During this time, just before the turn of the twentieth century, biblical artifacts mattered not only in academic circles but also for those who cared about the Bible as one of the central components of their faith.

Take, for example, the Revised Version of the Bible in Britain. Before this new version surfaced in 1881, the King James Bible was used almost exclusively by people of faith in England. But all that was about to change.

A scholar named Constantin von Tischendorf discovered an ancient biblical manuscript known as the Codex Sinaiticus in Saint Catherine's Monastery at Mount Sinai in 1844. The Codex Sinaiticus remains one of the most significant biblical manuscripts ever discovered. Commentators say the early Alexandrian Greek manuscript dates to the fourth century, was written on fine vellum, and originally contained the entire New Testament.[4] Tischendorf describes his remarkable find best:

> It was at the foot of Mount Sinai, in the convent of St. Catherine, that I discovered the pearl of all my researches. In visiting the library of the monastery, in the month of May, 1844, I perceived in the middle of the great hall a large and wide basket full of old parchments; and the librarian, who was a man of information, told me that two heaps of papers like this, mouldered by time, had been already committed to the flames.
>
> What was my surprise to find amid this heap of papers a considerable number of sheets of a copy of the Old Testament in Greek, which seemed to me to be one of the most ancient that I had ever seen. The authorities of the convent allowed me to possess myself of a third of these parchments, or about forty-five sheets, all the more readily as they were destined for the fire.
>
> But I could not get them to yield up possession of the remainder. The too lively satisfaction which I had displayed, had aroused their suspicions as to the value of this manuscript. I transcribed a page of the text of Isaiah and Jeremiah, and enjoined on the monks to take religious care of all such remains which might fall in their way.[5]

Cambridge scholars Brooke Westcott and Fenton Hort used this new ancient text—the Codex Sinaiticus—along with the highly secretive and prized Vatican texts, to finally produce a new version of the Bible that was based on these ancient and more recently found manuscripts.

This became the new Revised Version of the Bible. Many hoped it would put to rest much of the criticism leveled at the inconsistencies of the Greek manuscript on which the King James Bible was based. When the Revised Version was completed, Oxford University Press sold one million copies on the first day of its release.

Many of us don't know the history of our Bibles and take it for granted. Being people of faith and being in the Bible retail business, we cared about our Bibles, but we were not much different than anyone else. It wasn't until these trips that our interest in ancient biblical manuscripts and artifacts grew.

## Realizing the Power of an Artifact

Our understanding of the Bible and its known artifacts was expanding. It's not as if there are only one, two, or even ten artifacts. There are literally tens of thousands of them. Admittedly, they don't all carry the same amount of importance. They aren't all unparalleled manuscripts of antiquity that offer new insights into how Greek, Hebrew, and Aramaic are to be translated. But they do stack on top of each other, like the shelves of the library of history, offering us a mass compendium from which to learn. Each item adds a brick in the wall of evidence for the Bible.

We were seeing firsthand the reality that the Bible is so much more than a book for Westerners. It's a major world text with global influence.

CHAPTER 2

# A CODEX IN A CAT BASKET

*Your word is a lamp for my feet, a light on my path.*

—PSALM 119:105

*It is Christ Himself, not the Bible, who is the true word of God. The Bible, read in the right spirit and with the guidance of good teachers, will bring us to him.*

—C. S. LEWIS[1]

*He'l fear not what men say, / He'l labour Night and Day, / To be a Pilgrim.*

—JOHN BUNYAN, *THE PILGRIM'S PROGRESS*

When our contact made a trip to London, just a few months after our initial trip to Istanbul and Israel, he awaited the start of an auction for biblical artifacts at Christie's, a British auction house in London, while I was on the phone with him from Oklahoma City. We intended to bid on a manuscript of the book of Psalms translated into English by Richard Rolle (1290–1349).

Rolle was an interesting fellow. An English native, he dropped out of Oxford University to become a mystic and a hermit in Yorkshire.[2] Some believe his writings were read as widely as Chaucer's.

He is known for his work in Bible translation and biblical commentaries. This particular biblical manuscript, "The Roseberry Rolle, the Psalms and Canticles in pre-Wycliffite English translation, with the commentary of Richard Rolle," dates back to 1349—decades before Wycliffe's well-known translation of the Bible into English. It's speculated Rolle wrote this text for a fellow Yorkshire hermit, Margaret Kirkby, and that the original book was chained to his tomb.

Later in his life, Rolle moved to Richmondshire and "attended on the Cistercian nuns of Hampole until his death in 1349."[3] Rolle is credited with playing an influential role "in the formation of the religious culture of fifteenth-century England, and the number of extant manuscripts indicates that they were more widely read than those of any other vernacular writer."[4] Rolle's work influenced the followers of John Wycliffe, the Lollards, who represent his most enduring legacy.

Naturally, the availability of such an influential artifact was exciting. The suspense was building.

Our contact told me who else was in the room, and there were guesses as to who else might be on the other phone lines. As the auction began, we had to wait until the Rolle went up for bid. Once it came up for bid, the action began, and after just a few short minutes the gavel hit. We were the highest bidder. We acquired Rolle's piece. We were elated.

There had also been discussions with Sotheby's, another famous antiquities auction house in London. We wanted to know if they had any biblical items for us to consider as well. One item popped up. It was an artifact that had created some fuss months earlier. Seven months prior, in June of 2009, Westminster College at Cambridge University had put the famous Codex Climaci Rescriptus up for auction.

This was the manuscript the Scottish twin sisters Agnes and Margaret had found at Mount Sinai and had subsequently donated to Cambridge!

## What's in a Codex?

The Codex Climaci Rescriptus sounds like something out of a Dan Brown book. But rest assured, it's quite real, very important, and represents hundreds of years of biblical manuscript history. To understand why, you need to know the purpose of a codex and what it is.

Ancient writers used various types of writing instruments and wrote on different media: first clay tablets, then papyrus, and then parchment. Early ancient writers used papyrus (this is the origin of our English word *paper*), which was a kind of paper the Egyptians made from the papyrus plant that grew near the Nile. When thin strips of the plant were pressed together, perpendicular to one another, they would produce a natural glue to form the writing material, which could then be rolled into a scroll. Some scrolls could be extremely long. A lengthy New Testament book like the gospel of Matthew, for example, could roll out to over thirty feet.[5]

Early on, papyrus was the go-to writing material, and its popularity spread throughout the ancient Near East.[6] Parchment then became the popular writing material, around the second century BC, as it was more durable than papyrus. Parchment was made out of animal skin—goat, sheep, or cow—which would be scraped, stretched out over a frame, and dried to prepare it as a writing surface. It could be stitched together to form a scroll—and it still is today—or bound into a book form called a codex. An advantage of the codex was the ability to write on both sides of the writing surface. Also, it was much easier to flip through a book than to roll through a scroll. Parchment made from the skin of a young calf was called vellum. The younger the animal used for making the parchment, the better the quality of the writing surface.

The Codex Climaci Rescriptus, or CCR, is a codex written on vellum.[7] Some scholars suggest the more we discover about ancient writing, the more it appears the first Christians might be the ones responsible for the innovation of the codex.[8]

## The Mystery in the Cat Basket

The CCR contains a bit of mystery. The codex itself is referred to as a "rescriptus," which is also referred to as a "palimpsest." Basically, each page of the CCR contains multiple layers of writing. The top layer of the manuscript has been added, or written over text underneath. Now we're able to unlock more of those mysteries. Part of the underlying text is visible and can be read unaided, but much is unreadable. With new scanning technology, we are able to determine what more of the underlying text says.

The original cat basket in which the CCR was presented to us.

The top text is a writing entitled "Ladder of Divine Ascent" by the abbot of the monastery at Mount Sinai, John Climacus. His original writing was in Greek, but this copy is a translation in Syriac.

With scanning technology that was being developed at Oxford, called Multi-Spectral Imaging, we were able to pull out the underlying text while making the top text disappear. Most of the underlying text is biblical, in an Aramaic language. These new scans were then taken to scholars at Cambridge for translation.

It's interesting how things come back around. An artifact previously held by Westminster College at Cambridge University, given up at auction, now finds its way back to the university for renewed research.

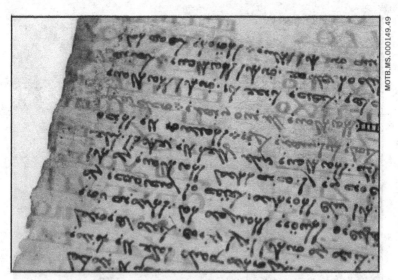

The Codex Climaci Rescriptus, Sinai, Egypt,
6th–10th century (Museum of the Bible).

The CCR represented a huge find. In the biblical artifact world, this was like acquiring a Monet, if you could pull it off. With the economic crash of 2008, many institutions, even in England, felt the financial squeeze.

We couldn't believe our luck. The auctioneers told us that last June (2009), the CCR was placed in an auction—an auction for Western manuscripts. This auction did not necessarily attract collectors of biblical artifacts. So the CCR did not meet the minimum bid.

Now we were asking if the representatives at Sotheby's had anything in which we might be interested. That's when we were informed of the CCR. Sotheby's still had the manuscript under contract; we negotiated for it and were able to acquire it.

The adventure of it all had sucked us in. We could see now how important and monumental these artifacts were. That's a humbling and sobering thing. Very quickly the world of biblical manuscript collecting was impacting our own faith. We had grown up with the

Bible. It was a book we had learned from when we were young. Our parents lived by the principles in it, and we endeavored to do the same. And now that object, that book on our shelf or nightstand, took on new meaning. In many ways, it somehow became more intimate to us.

Something beautiful happens when you see manuscripts from the second and third centuries. As we have displayed items at exhibits around the country and around the world, we have often been told how impactful seeing an actual item can be.

You feel the history in a personal way. A way that's impossible to experience when you simply download your Bible online (usually for free), purchase it on the internet, or buy a printed copy in a store. Like so many in America, we learned our ethics and the deep truths of our faith through the Bible. And like so many others in the world, our personal story enhances our encounter with such a book.

CHAPTER 3

# THE JOURNEY
# BEYOND ISTANBUL

*The unfolding of your words gives light; / it gives understanding to the simple.*

—PSALM 119:130

*I only know enough of God to want to worship him, by any means ready to hand.*

—ANNIE DILLARD, *HOLY THE FIRM*

*[A]nd he told me a story. Or rather, since Christians are so fond of capital letters, a Story. And what a story. The first thing that drew me in was disbelief. What? It's humanity's sins but it's God's son who pays the price?*

—YANN MARTEL, *LIFE OF PI*

Sometimes it's the unassuming gesture that makes the most profound impact on your life. We never set out to build a museum for the Bible. We were happy raising our children and helping to run the family business. We were still thinking that someone else was going to put the museum together, and we were content to help keep the items safe, then donate them to the museum. Little did we know that when we agreed to help acquire a biblical artifact, our future had changed.

We had to ask ourselves, "What would it look like for us to keep the dream alive and work toward building a museum to house all these wonderful ancient biblical artifacts?" That thought was, honestly, overwhelming.

But the deeper question we had to ask and answer for ourselves was, "What does it mean for us to take this journey?" The answer to that question is the premise for this book. It's an answer that unfolds like an archaeological dig, layers upon layers removed until the experience of discovery makes us smile in delight.

We discovered how precious these artifacts are. They are also precious to all kinds of people, all over the world. So many people of different faith traditions have pulled us aside and expressed their gratitude for this project. It's one of the most rewarding aspects of our journey in building a museum. We've found a remarkable sense of unity around this ancient text. That excites and inspires us.

Holding up the Bible as this wonderful human treasure invites people of all walks of life to come and see, explore, and discover this gift of history. It is astounding that so many people from different parts of the world—people of different cultures, ethnicities, ages, and languages—all meet up around one book that was written thousands of years ago.

At the same time, we recognize that today in America, the Bible does not possess the same centrality that it did at our country's founding. Journalist and author Kenneth Briggs observes, "For more and more Americans, the Bible has become a museum exhibit, hallowed as a treasure but enigmatic and untouched. Snippets of its languages still pop up occasionally in political speeches. But overall, the Bible is overridden by consumer appetites and a growing array of lifestyles that . . . offer ways of thinking about life, love, and work that have left the Bible behind."[1]

We believe, however, that this is only partially true of our culture. It may be that we are simply not as skeptical as Mr. Briggs, but our observation is that yes, although our culture does not know the Bible as it once did, there is real longing to know it better. We can all, as a nation and as collective humanity, observe, appreciate, study, and discuss this book. So much wonder and mystery surrounds not only the Bible itself, as a cultural artifact, but also its claims, its narrative, and its ultimate message.

## Retailers, Not Collectors

Before we go farther, let's pause to look at a word we keep throwing around as if we all know what it entails when we use it about the Bible: artifact. The word artifact comes to us from the science of archaeology. And, for our journey, biblical archaeology remains the specific field of archaeology that focuses on discovering "objects that have survived from the past"[2] that relate to the Bible and its history, people, customs, and basically its culture.

As people, we discover and sometimes keep objects that have survived from the past. They might not be a piece of crumbling papyrus or an ancient codex in a cat basket. Our artifacts often take the forms of memories. Sometimes those memories look like photographs or a special gift from a special friend. Other times they're simply the bits of our lives we carry in us that form who we are today. The memories we accumulate reveal the winding road our individual paths, our journeys, our lives, have taken.

And it's not as if our memories come packaged. Life happens one moment at a time and leads often to places we never thought it would.

The Bible chronicles the journeys of many different characters. But the Bible's claim is the telling of a story that is one long journey—the journey of humanity's relationship with God. Biblical artifacts tell the story of the copying and printing of manuscripts over thousands of years. And the collected stories that fill the pages of the Bible act like artifacts of a personal journey to which we can all relate: of love, failure, grace, and redemption.

Our memories act powerfully. They can remind us of good times as well as bad. They can transport us to places where we can almost make out the smells and tastes of times past. The great twentieth-century writer and Oxford professor C. S. Lewis knew the power of memory. He described his conversion from atheism to Christianity as a religious journey. He found himself in a place familiar; he remembered it—like he had been there before and was returning from exile. For Lewis, memories acted like signposts of home, that place he was supposed to be.

Our journey with the museum reminds us how God leads us with a journey in mind. We were working for our family business and trying to help some others in their worthy endeavor.

As the collection grew, the family started feeling the responsibility of it. We had been entrusted with the items, and we felt we needed to be sure the dream of a museum became a reality. The idea was not new to the family; my brother had mentioned more than once over the years the idea of building a Bible museum. He was building a chain of Christian bookstores and carried one of the largest selections of Bibles available. So little by little, we embraced the dream.

One of the first ideas as a result was opening a traveling exhibit. I (Steve) have said that we, my family, are not collectors. My dad operates by the philosophy that if you buy a new shirt, an old shirt has to go. We were acquiring artifacts not because we were collectors but because we wanted to tell their story.

The problem was, our closet was getting full, and we had no idea when we would be opening a museum. We had no location or date; it was only a dream at the time. That's when the idea for a traveling exhibit was birthed. We could start telling the incredible story of the items we had acquired, while the idea of the museum developed.

Toward the end of 2010, we had a two-day planning meeting for a Bible exhibit. We wanted to open the exhibit in 2011, launching it with the celebration of the four-hundredth anniversary of the King James Version of the Bible. The King James Version is the most printed version of the Bible, and we thought that would be a great opportunity to launch an exhibit.

In 2011, we successfully opened our U.S. version of a traveling exhibit at the Oklahoma City Museum of Art.

This was the beginning of a journey, a journey with an unknown destination. Not too long after we opened the Oklahoma City exhibit, through some contacts at American Bible Society, discussions began about having an exhibit at the Vatican. We had just finished a race to open the first exhibit, and now the race was on again, as the desired opening for the exhibit at the Vatican was during the lenten season of

2012. We successfully opened the U.S. exhibit for the lenten season, which was the first of other international exhibits to come.

Before the museum opened, we had also traveled to Jerusalem, Argentina, Cuba, and Germany. We also traveled to several universities across the U.S., with exhibits of varying sizes.

Over the next five years, the U.S. exhibit traveled to five cities total, with its last tour ending in 2016 in Santa Clarita, California. It had grown from a fifteen-thousand-square-foot exhibit in Oklahoma City to a forty-thousand-square-foot exhibit before it was closed.

Back in 2011, none of this had been in sight.

We can only see so far. We can only do the work before us. But if this process has taught us anything, it's to stay alert; there's a master plan at play.

At this point in our journey, we also felt a great sense of anticipation. The more we learned about biblical artifacts, the more excited we grew. The more people we met who voiced their joy about the project, the more our hearts grew for the project of creating a museum. There's something about the Bible. People want to know about it. They want to own a copy. They want to understand it more. And they want it kept safe forever.

## To Explore Is to See

We humans are naturally curious. Even the word curious piques our interest. When we read it or hear someone use it, don't we want to know what's going on?

Curious about what?

Historians call the time between the fifteenth century and the eighteenth century the Age of Exploration. As a country, we are most familiar with a certain character from that age: Christopher Columbus. Columbus worked at the pleasure of the Spanish monarchs and took on one of the world's most popular exploration adventures. He sought the New World.[3]

The world boomed with new commerce during this time. Capitalism spread its wings as the race to build empires took hold of world powers like Spain, England, and France. This economic activity spurred growth and exploration.

But what about the human spirit?

We possess a natural inclination to *know*. And to know, we must go. We must experience the thrill of discovering something new.

Today, if we want to know something, we ask our digital devices a question. Christopher Columbus had to board a ship and take on the ravages of sailing the Atlantic Ocean—disease, violence, the elements. He had to make a commitment to go, and to go on, and to keep going even though the end of the journey was unknown.

And what did Columbus and his crew see in their journey? Some days, no doubt, they saw little. The only thing that carried them was their determination, and the anticipation of what lay ahead.

Anticipation can wield great power. It's a natural ally to exploration and adventure. It fuels our curiosity. Even when we can't see the journey's end, we carry on with hope and anticipate the reward of the adventure. That's the beauty of exploration. And that was our experience. Anticipation led us along the journey.

So, as we've said, people want to know. They want to discover. They want to explore. And to explore is to see. It is to play with an idea until it becomes a reality. It's to look at things from a different perspective.

The Bible embodies the characteristics of exploration. Its history intrigues us. Its storytelling captivates us. Its message stuns us. It is a compendium of memories from the past we need to preserve, and it has played a part in our own journeys. It touches most people in some way, either directly or indirectly. It beckons us to come and see.

As our anticipation grew, so did our collection. As we continued to acquire artifacts, we realized this little project was already much bigger than us. It possessed the potential to draw the curiosity of so many others. And, like anything you care about and pour time and energy into, it becomes part of you. The collection has become something very special to our entire family. Even our children contribute to the dream now.

It is human nature to greatly value the things in which we invest ourselves—our time, our talents, our treasures. We believe that's what Jesus means in Matthew 6:21 and Luke 12:34: "Where your treasure is, there your heart will be also."

Exploration tends to inspire more exploration. When you find something interesting, as you start digging, you don't mind digging a little more. We hope that's true in the next chapter as we give you a mountaintop tour of the Bible. We want to show you a book full of wonder and goodness—and danger.

# PART 2

# THE BOOK

יָבֵשׁ חָצִיר

*The grass withers and the flowers fall, but the word of our God
endures forever.*

—ISAIAH 40:8

*Whenever we feel that there is something odd in Christian theology,
we shall generally find that there is something odd in the truth.*

—G. K. CHESTERTON, *ORTHODOXY*

# CHAPTER 4

# BOOK OF WONDER: THE STORY OF THE BIBLE

*The existence of the Bible, as a book for the people, is the greatest benefit which the human race has ever experienced. Every attempt to belittle it is a crime against humanity.*

—IMMANUEL KANT[1]

*Jesus did many other things as well. If every one of them were written down, I suppose that even the whole world would not have room for the books that would be written.*

—JOHN 21:25

*Lord, what a book, what lessons! What a book is the Holy Scripture, what a miracle, what powers are given to man with it! Like a carven image of the world, and of man, and of human characters, and everything is named and set forth unto ages of ages.*

—ELDER ZOSIMA, *THE BROTHERS KARAMAZOV*

*A book, too, can be a star, "explosive material, capable of stirring up fresh life endlessly," a living fire to lighten the darkness, leading out into the expanding universe.*

—MADELEINE L'ENGLE[2]

What is the Bible?

Sure, it looks like a book that millions and millions of people keep on a shelf in their house. Research shows over 80 percent of Americans own a hard copy of the Bible. More than half of agnostics and skeptics own a Bible.

But have you ever asked, "What is this book, really?"

If you dig around, you'll find that many authors explain the Bible as a collection of books written by over forty authors, in three languages, over fifteen hundred years.[3] Interesting, yes, but even that explanation just describes the Bible as a book written by several people. Those facts describe *how* the Bible was written, but fail to describe the what. *What* is the Bible?

We want to go another route.

A friend of ours told us the Bible is like a cabinet of wonder. We had no idea what he was talking about. But after he explained it, it made more sense. What did he mean by "cabinet of wonder"? Here's what he told us.

During the European Renaissance—the rebirth of art and literature in the fourteenth century—rulers, aristocrats, merchants, and scientists curated cabinets of wonder, or *wunderkammers* (pronounced "voonder-calmer"). These wonder cabinets foreshadowed our modern-day museums. Curators filled them with religious relics, items of natural history, works of art, and antiquities.[4] Well, we like the connection of wonder cabinets to museums.

Our friend continued telling us how some writers today refer to blogs as the twenty-first-century version of the *wunderkammer*. When you think about all the information on the internet and how blogs and curated newsletters attempt to cobble together different pockets of information for specific uses, it's not too much of a stretch.

Think about Google's mission. They want to organize all the information in the world and make it accessible. All the knowledge of the world, right at our fingertips. Google works like a supercharged table of contents. You can literally search any person, topic, or event in the world at any time and see images, photographs, or articles about it. Google works like a massive cabinet of wonder and invites us to explore. On a micro level, blogs organize the content even further.

How is the Bible like a *wunderkammer*, or cabinet of wonder?

The idea is to view the Bible as a sort of scrapbook. Except instead of photographs of family and close friends, we find a curated cabinet of stories, laws, poetry, wisdom literature, and letters. The wonder of it all comes not just from the breadth of content but also from the length of time it took to collect it all, the coherence of the pieces, and the timelessness of the wisdom.

The idea of the Bible as a cabinet of wonder was quite fitting. It seemed appropriate because, just like the Renaissance cabinets of wonder that foreshadowed museums, the Bible acts as a sort of ancient Near East museum of priceless manuscripts. It collects timeless stories and wraps them in one of the most beautiful and controversial stories ever told.

It tells the story of a God, who created the universe, and of humankind, expelled from the garden by choosing their own way and then later pursued through the man Jesus of Nazareth. It chronicles how God reaches to humankind through a people, a law, and prophets.

The wonder cabinet is a fun way to look at the Bible. And even though the analogy is not how we normally look at or talk about the Bible, it does make some nice connections to the Bible as a mini-museum as well as a book that contains different literary genres and stories of wonder, amazement, and intrigue.

## The Bible Is a Story

Stories have been used throughout time as vehicles for truth. Even today, every culture passes down its history and values through storytelling. Everyone loves a good movie—for its storyline. Stories can cut through biased assumptions and ignite our imaginations. Stories don't prescribe doctrine. They engage the heart. For a story to exist, it must be told. And that's what the Bible does. It tells.

If we're to read the Bible as a story, then we need to be careful that we don't pick and choose what we want, cutting out snippets for our own personal needs. Stories demand our entire attention and require us to read them in full, or we may miss an important detail. It is also important that we accurately understand what the stories teach. We are told in the Bible that we are to "rightly [handle] the word of truth" (2 Tim. 2:15 ESV). This means we do not have the right to say it means whatever we want it to mean, but we must seek to understand the lesson it is trying to teach. In other words, it's important that we take an honest approach to the lessons and stories found in the book.

The Bible has a beginning, a middle, and an end. It has characters, plot twists, and themes. Each story in the Bible contributes to the grand story, what we like to call the biblical narrative, and should be read with this big story in mind. If we read the stories in isolation and without context, we lose so much of what the story is telling us.

As with all stories, we find so much packed into the pages. We find beauty, mystery, war, suffering, victory, redemption, betrayal, love, hate, death, and life. Each of these elements holds true whether we believe the Bible or not.

The Bible is filled with people. It tells the stories of families, friends, nations, kings, queens, sons, daughters, fathers, and mothers.

The Bible is filled with poetry and song. People the world over look to the longest book in the Bible, Psalms, for encouragement, peace, and healing, or to the book of Proverbs for the nuggets of wisdom it contains.

When you stop and consider the amazing reality that the most famous book the world has ever seen is a collection of small stories that tell an even bigger story, you must marvel.

The Bible starts with an incredible line. It says, "In the beginning God created the heavens and the earth" (Gen. 1:1). Right from the start, we are faced with questions. What are we to think? Is there a God? Are we to believe what is written? Can any of this be true? From its first sentence, the Bible sets forth the existence of God as a self-evident fact. At the end of God's creation work, the Bible says, he pronounced his work "good."

Shortly thereafter we read the story of man's disobedience. We encounter the story of Adam and Eve and learn how the serpent deceived them in the garden and how they broke God's one rule: don't eat from the Tree of Knowledge of Good and Evil. That was the only restriction man was given. Without that tree, there was no way for man to disobey and therefore no way to choose to obey or to love. This was the original religious freedom!

The Bible says that we are created in God's image, and one of the unique aspects of humankind is our ability to choose, to love or not to love, because love requires a choice. The tree was God's way of giving man choice. Man was told a lie, and because he believed the lie, he chose to disobey. That disobedience created a separation between God and man. The result can be seen in the chaos that followed. Death and destruction, culminating in the flood.

Imagine for a moment that it is springtime and you decide to do some spring cleaning. You send the kids out to play, and after a valiant effort, you are able to perfectly clean your house so that there is not a speck of dust; everything has a place, and everything is in its place. A real dream come true! Now you have a problem: you can't let your children in the house. As soon as they step foot inside the house, it is no longer perfectly clean. That is the claim of the Bible. Because of our disobedience, our sin, we are no longer able to connect with God as we were created to connect. His perfection demands separation. It is this problem that the story goes on to deal with.

Then we learn about the birth and life of the nation of Israel. This section packs a punch; it's loaded with stories of war and miracles. The story of Abraham disturbs and dazzles us—God tells Abraham to sacrifice his only son, and just as Abraham lifts his knife to kill his son on the altar of sacrifice, an angel stops him and shows him a ram stuck in a nearby thicket to sacrifice instead. Pretty intense drama!

We read about the extraordinary life of Moses. He is orphaned, then raised as a son to Pharaoh, living the life of royalty. After murdering an Egyptian for beating a Jew, Moses flees to the wilderness, where God appears to him in a bush that burns yet is not consumed by the fire. There God calls Moses to lead his people, the Jews, out of Egyptian slavery and into a promised land. This is the stuff movies are made of! Moses accomplishes this but endures great challenge and peril. He is responsible for the most heralded event in Jewish history—the Exodus from Egypt, which is still commemorated to this day as Passover.

We also read about the young and handsome shepherd boy, David. David is one of the more popular figures in all the Bible. He's described as "a man after [God's] own heart" (1 Sam. 13:14). David's story is so epic that it requires a quick telling.

David is just minding his business, tending sheep, when his father asks him to take food to his older brothers, who are serving the king in battle. When David arrives at the front lines to deliver their food, he hears the nine-foot-tall champion from the enemy camp mocking God and the Israelites.

Offended, David asks the Israelites, "What's in it for the man who kills that Philistine and gets rid of this ugly blot on Israel's honor? Who does he think he is, anyway, this uncircumcised Philistine, taunting the armies of God?"

So the king lets David confront the giant Philistine champion. When David approaches Goliath, the giant looks at him and says, "Come on, I'll make roadkill of you for the buzzards. I'll turn you into a tasty morsel for the field mice." No, really, that is really the way the Bible puts this.

But David is not deterred. He replies, "You come at me with sword and spear and battle-ax. I come at you in the name of GOD-of-the-Angel-Armies."[5]

Then he takes his sling and whips a smooth stone at Goliath, hitting him in the forehead. The giant falls, and David grabs the giant's mammoth sword and removes his head.

More stuff of movies!

There are stories of heroines like Ruth and Esther showing great courage, of prophets warning of God's punishment because of disobedience, and of repentance and rebuilding after years of captivity. Each story teaches lessons itself, and yet each is a piece of a larger picture.

Then we read about a certain carpenter from Nazareth, Jesus, son of Mary. Jesus enters the scene when the nation of Israel waits to hear from God. Jesus arrives and says controversial things. His actions match his words, and he is quickly embraced by hordes of people because he heals them and eats and drinks with those considered to be the lowliest people in town.

How does he heal them? He speaks to them. He tells one young paralyzed man to pick up his mat and walk. And the man does! For a blind man, Jesus spits into dirt and makes mud, then puts the mud on the blind man's eyes. Sight!

Another man, an invalid for thirty-eight years, has been sitting by a "healing pool" for a long time. But when Jesus sees him, Jesus asks if he wants to be healed. The man replies with a story about how he can never get into the healing pool quickly enough. Jesus replies, "Get up, take up your bed, and walk" (John 5:8 ESV). He walks!

Jesus shows up late to his friend's house and discovers that he's been dead for days. Overcome with grief, Jesus weeps.

Then he asks the locals to open up the tomb. The people fear the foul stench of the dead body but open the tomb. Jesus shouts to his friend, "Lazarus, come out" (John 11:43 ESV). His close friend rises from the dead and walks out of the tomb, grave clothes still wrapped around him. Jesus' path is strewn with miracles.

He claims to be the Messiah—just what the Israelites are waiting for! A national leader. But he disappoints many because he does not want to overthrow the oppressive Roman government. Instead he talks about a kingdom that is "not of this world" (John 18:36).

He talks about how he came to bring eternal life to the world by dying and coming back to life in three days. It's crazy talk for this no-name son of a carpenter. Or is it? He claims to be the fulfillment of all the Law and the Prophets! He claims to be the one to fix the sin problem that has been there from the beginning. Believe it or not—you must read the story!

The name of Jesus stirs people up. Most people, including historians, admit that a man named Jesus walked the earth and was indeed killed in the fashion depicted in the Bible. But Jesus' words present a scandal. He claimed to be the Son of God (Matt. 26:63–64), the giver of eternal life (John 10:28), the one who forgives sins (Mark 2:10), the Bread of Life (John 6:35), the Light of the World (John 8:12), and the Savior, because he died for man's wrong choice (John 3:14–16).

Most scandalous of all, Jesus says, "I am the way and the truth and the life. No one comes to the Father except through me" (John 14:6). What do we do with such a claim? How do we fit this claim into our pluralistic society? Jesus, as a character in this Bible's narrative, demands our attention. His life and resurrection stories are narratives worth exploring. His claims, if true, require more than attention; they require some kind of response: belief or disbelief.

After Jesus' ascension into heaven, we read from the likes of Peter and John, two of Jesus' most beloved friends and disciples. We also read from the pen of Paul, a former persecutor of Christians. Luke, the writer of the book of Acts, records Paul's dramatic conversion, when Jesus appears to Paul in blinding light. The light blinds Paul for days, as he finds his way to Damascus. A disciple of Jesus heals Paul after Jesus speaks to the disciple through a dream.

Having regained his sight, Paul heads straight for Peter and John and learns the teachings of Jesus. After his dramatic conversion, this former Christian-killer now follows Jesus and ends up writing most of the New Testament.

Here again, historians recognize there was a man named Paul, a follower of Jesus.

The Bible ends with an epic book that describes what life will be like in the end of days. John, who some refer to as "the beloved disciple," wrote the book of Revelation. In this last book of the Bible, he encounters an angel from God who shows him what will happen in the last days before and after Jesus returns for a second time, to collect his followers and to banish evil once and for all.

Revelation is a book cloaked in controversy and outlandish interpretations. But for those who follow this Jesus, it also possesses advice and encouragement.

## Jackie's Findings in the Bible

When I think about the incredible story told in the Bible, I've had to ask how it applies to my life. I can't help thinking about all the millions, even billions, of people who have read those stories and identified with them in some way. That has been my experience as well. I've leaned into the stories of the Bible for comfort many times, and I use what I know of the Bible as a guide for my own life.

I remember, it was early in our marriage. I was barely nineteen. Things got hard quick for Steve and me as newlyweds. Steve made some bold but—in hindsight—unfortunate financial decisions just before we married. He purchased his brother's house to use as an investment property. But he didn't know the oil industry was about to go bust.

At one point in that first year of marriage, we owned two homes, and only one of us had a paycheck coming in. Making two house payments each month at twenty-one and nineteen years old was a tough way to begin a marriage. I began working part-time at the office as a buyer's assistant to help pay the bills. We did what we could to keep our heads above water. It was a hard time.

How did I remain caring and steadfast for my husband as my world unraveled? Whatever preconceived notions I had entertained regarding marriage faded into a reality that pushed me to the comfort of the Bible's promises.

Many nights I felt overcome, so I slipped out of bed in the quiet of the night and walked over to our other bedroom and just stared out the window and cried. I cried and cried. What was I doing? Would we be okay? How could we make more money? Could we sell the other house and get that weight off us?

So in the middle of the night, I sat down in that quiet room and opened my Bible. I read different passages of Scripture that resonated with my feelings, and I allowed my eyes and my heart to soak in the words. The more I read, the more comfort I felt. This was my lifeline. I read until my heart settled. Then I bowed my head and prayed. I prayed for Steve. I prayed for us.

Then I silently slipped into bed.

The Bible's stories, and the Bible's story, enrich our lives with a peace you can only attempt to explain. Our lives weave in and out of good times and hard times. Every single one of us has those times; nobody is immune to difficulties in life. The question is, how do we handle them?

Using the Bible as a guidebook for all things that come our way works every time. For me, it didn't make my problems go away, but it sure did help me sort through and figure out what my part was in working through things.

In those early years, the Bible's promises and message of hope spoke to me. It breathed life into me and comforted me. It stitched itself into my life—into our lives.

CHAPTER 5

# MORE THAN A BOOK

*"Heaven and earth will pass away, but my words will never pass away."*

—MATTHEW 24:35

*And yet just because it is a book about both the sublime and the unspeakable, it is a book also about life the way it really is. It is a book about people who at one and the same time can be both believing and unbelieving, innocent and guilty, crusaders and crooks, full of hope and full of despair. In other words it is a book about us.*

—FREDERICK BUECHNER,
*WISHFUL THINKING*

*And God said, You are worth more to me / than one hundred sparrows. / And when I read that, I wept. / And God said, Whom have I blessed more than I have blessed you?*

—TONY HOAGLAND, "BIBLE STUDY"

If you do a Google search for the bestselling books of all time, you'll find several competing lists. Some lists have J. R. R. Tolkien's *The Lord of the Rings* trilogy as selling over 150 million copies, with his book *The Hobbit* not far behind. J. K. Rowling's *Harry Potter and the Philosopher's Stone* and the classic *The Little Princess* have both sold more than 100 million copies.

Then there's Dan Brown's *The Da Vinci Code* and C. S. Lewis's *The Lion, The Witch and the Wardrobe*—an interesting pairing!—easing in at around 80 million each. One website had Cervantes's *Don Quixote* at over 150 million. Really? We couldn't believe that. Then there's *The Catcher in the Rye* at 65 million and *Black Beauty* at 50 million. We think our daughters will be happy to hear that *Black Beauty* made the list.

We found pastor Rick Warren's book *The Purpose Driven Life* listed at 30 million, but we feel like that book *has* to be up there with Cervantes's, right? *The Tale of Peter Rabbit, Gone with the Wind, The Hunger Games, To Kill a Mockingbird, Charlotte's Web, War and Peace, The Wind in the Willows, The Girl with the Dragon Tattoo*—the list of bestsellers goes on and on, each one selling tens of millions. It's quite impressive. And interesting to see the diverse literature that has shaped past and current culture.

Now consider this.

The Bible is the bestselling book every year and of *all time*. Let that sink in for a moment. Even more than *The Lord of the Rings*? Yes. *The Guinness Book of World Records* estimates that between 1815 and 1975 over 2.5 billion—that's billion with a B—Bibles were printed, sold, or distributed. Now estimates reach beyond 5 billion. Tolkien and Rowling have some catching up to do.

What about translating the bestselling books into other languages? Again, the numbers vary.

*Alice's Adventures in Wonderland* translated into 97 languages. The Qur'an, 112 languages. *Andersen's Fairy Tales*? 153 languages. *Twenty Thousand Leagues Under the Sea* submarines in at 174 languages. John Bunyan's *The Pilgrim's Progress* comes in at a whopping 200 languages. Some claim the second most translated text in history is *The Adventures of Pinocchio*: 260 languages!

Just to give you context, there are approximately 5,800 vital languages in the world. The complete Bible has been translated into over 650 of those languages. The New Testament has been translated into over 1,500 more, making over 2,150 languages with at least the New Testament! Some experts think that with the current effort that is underway, every vital language will possess at least the New Testament of the Bible by the year 2033. No other book comes close.

Now think about how accessible the Bible is, not only to us here in the United States but also to people throughout the rest of the world. In America, we have the luxury of choosing from a variety of English Bible versions. Over 80 percent of all American households own a Bible; over 70 percent have at least two Bibles. How many of us can remember receiving our first Bible from a loved one?

And how many of us have *YouVersion* (the Bible app) downloaded on our phones? Now, in the twenty-first century, anyone in the world who owns a smartphone can possess a free version of the Bible. Since *YouVersion* launched in 2008, it has been one of the most downloaded apps in history, with over one thousand languages supported, and it contains audio versions in hundreds of languages.

The vast reach of the Bible is staggering. What does that say about our interest, even hunger, for this book? What is it that draws so many people to it?

## A Very Present Help

As with many people of faith, there are times when I (Jackie) couldn't tell you a reference for where a verse is in the Bible, but I know many passages from the Bible. For example, "Lo, I am with you always, even unto the end of the world." This verse is one that is always in the storehouse of my mind. I have heard the Scriptures my whole life, since I started attending church when I was a tiny baby. It was prevalent in my home life as well. When you grow up with it, it becomes a part of you and is woven into your identity.

Even if I don't recall the scriptural references from my years of growing up in an atmosphere of Bible followers, many readings and different passages have stuck with me. It wasn't like we could pull out our mobile device and look something up, using a search tool.

We read the Scriptures from a printed copy of the Bible, so if you wanted to look up a verse, you had to check the concordance in the back of the book. The concordance is like an index of topics referenced in the Bible. Another option was to pull out a *Strong's Concordance*, which we have today on our bookshelf. This is an in-depth tool that references everywhere in the Bible that a particular word is used. Every word is referenced, including *a*, *the*, and *I*. I can't imagine why anyone would want to know every verse in the Bible that uses the word *the*. People rarely have to go about it this way now, which I believe is an amazing gift to us. We now can search any topic or verse or word at the touch of a fingertip on a device that so many of us carry everywhere we go.

When you are a young mother to four kids (with two more kids to come), you cling to encouragement in whatever form you can find. Steve and I got married at the ripe old ages of twenty and eighteen. We had our first child when I was twenty years old, and our fourth child came along by the time I was twenty-seven.

During that time in my life, the Twenty-Third Psalm spoke to me. A psalm is a Hebrew poem, written with the expectation of being sung. The book of Psalms, found in the Old Testament of the Bible, contains 150 different psalms. It is the longest book in the Bible. King David, whom we referenced earlier as the shepherd boy who killed a giant, wrote most of it.

I remember as I would go to sleep at night, I would quote the entire Twenty-Third Psalm and feel peace.

> The LORD is my shepherd; I shall not want.
> He maketh me to lie down in green pastures: he leadeth me beside the still waters.
> He restoreth my soul: he leadeth me in the paths of righteousness for his name's sake.
> Yea, though I walk through the valley of the shadow of death, I will fear no evil: for thou art with me; thy rod and thy staff they comfort me.
> Thou preparest a table before me in the presence of mine enemies: thou anointest my head with oil; my cup runneth over.
> Surely goodness and mercy shall follow me all the days of my life: and I will dwell in the house of the LORD for ever.
>
> —PSALM 23 KJV

That psalm reminded me that God was with me and he cared (as a shepherd) for me. When I meditated on him and read the Bible, he brought peace and restoration to my soul.

If I needed strength, he gave it.

If I needed guidance, he was the answer in all areas of my life. He provided for me and my entire family. He would always be with me and walk beside me.

Those promises meant the world to me as a young mother with a house full of small children.

Then, when I was twenty-nine years old, I awoke one morning, and as soon as I got up, I noticed that my feet hurt really bad.

*What's going on?* I thought.

I got up and walked around. Maybe the pain would stop if I kept moving. I noticed that my feet were red and swollen.

After a couple weeks of this, with the pain never completely going away, I mentioned it to Steve.

"Maybe you should go to the doctor and have it checked out," he said.

So I did, and I began a journey of trying different nonsteroidal medications to help with the inflammation.

It didn't make any difference. I really didn't like taking medications, and it only got worse.

It's really hard to take care of four little kids (ages one, three, five, and seven) when you are dealing with so much physical pain. Add in homeschooling our five- and seven-year-olds on top of the daily workload, and each day seemed to be a daunting task.

Steve's work required that he travel more and more. Plus, I no longer lived near my mother, and Steve's mom traveled quite a bit and worked at the Hobby Lobby corporate offices. I didn't feel like I could give in to my body's demand for rest.

When the medications failed to help, I took it hard.

*The Lord is my shepherd. He cares for me.*

The refrain of hope ran through my mind, even as I kept asking myself, *What is going on?*

Fear crept into my life during this time. I struggled with it. I had never been *really* sick in my life. With all of the things I tried to balance, I felt overwhelmed. I would crumple into bed at night, exhausted and in constant pain.

The fear of the unknown was the worst. I didn't know whether I would ever feel good again or whether my life was going to be much shorter than I expected. I didn't know what to do. I had no recourse. I felt trapped, and it was all I could do not to panic.

More tests. More appointments. More pain.

I knew I had to try to keep life as normal as possible for my precious children. I didn't want my fear and anxiety to rub off on them.

I wanted my children to have a mother who was all in—not one who was emotionally frozen with fear.

Finally, the doctors made a diagnosis: rheumatoid arthritis.

I didn't know anything about it. I wasn't familiar with anyone who had it. I had many questions running through my mind.

*How did I develop an autoimmune disease?*

*What does this mean for the rest of my life?*

*How do I deal with this?*

*How am I going to take care of my children and my responsibilities?*

*How will I cope with the pain and still hang on to my joy, not letting it get me down?*

But it did get me down.

One night I got alone in the house (which was hard to do) and poured my heart out to God. I said, "God, I just need a verse that I can stand on. A verse to quote anytime the worry, the pain, and the fear threaten to overtake me." I found a verse in the Bible that gave me great comfort in a different way than the psalm: "We know that all things work together for good to them that love God, to them who are the called according to his purpose" (Rom. 8:28 KJV).

I would quote it when I was going to sleep at night. I'd quote it anytime I was feeling overwhelmed during the day. There was a long season when I just clung to that verse.

I knew God could make something good come out of this bad situation. If I was going to be sick, I wanted to make sure I learned valuable lessons through the difficult times, and that my husband and children did too.

In my mind, the good would be the valuable life lessons we would learn. The difficult times taught me to be more compassionate toward those who had it worse than me and to be more grateful for the good things, the blessings in my life. I tried to do everything that I knew of to be healthier.

I was advised to get a lot of rest. How do you get a lot of rest with a house full of healthy, rambunctious children you are responsible for? All of the searching for natural treatments, different doctors, different tests, more vitamins, and the cure-all remedy was time consuming. I didn't have the energy to keep looking for and trying new things.

It was exhausting.

I knew that people prayed for me. My family, Steve's family, our friends—everybody was praying. They gave me so much support. Nobody knew what to do to really help, other than to pray and let me know they were standing with me and believed in God's healing power with me. We knew that he could heal me instantly, but he wasn't at that time.

Until he did, I needed to hang on to my joy and my faith.

I had to move forward and not let the new circumstances change who I was, and I had to know that I wasn't going to be going through it alone. I had a loving husband and my dear children. I had a lot to be happy about and grateful for. It was still tough.

I clung to the Word.

There were a lot of times when I would write Bible verses on index cards and keep them close to me.

I kept them in my purse, nearby, giving me a sense of peace.

I kept my index cards with Scriptures in my nightstand and would regularly pull them out and read them just before going to sleep at night. I wanted to have my thoughts full of God's thoughts as I drifted off to sleep.

Many days I felt like I could either laugh or cry. I would say, "I look a lot better when I'm laughing than I do when I'm crying, so I'm going to laugh!"

The verses that helped me embrace laughter were, "A joyful heart is good medicine" (Prov. 17:22 ESV) and "A happy heart makes the face cheerful, but heartache crushes the spirit" (Prov. 15:13).

I was determined to "rejoice in the Lord always" (Phil. 4:4), no matter what came my way. This was like medicine to my heart and soul. Even though the physical pain was still there, I began to take the walk out of the "valley of the shadow of death" that had caused me such fear, distress, and worry. I felt like God was walking beside me all the way. He would never leave me. The darkness could never overcome me when I kept my eyes fixed on him.

He was my light.

"The LORD is my light and my salvation; whom shall I fear? The LORD is the strength of my life; of whom [or what] shall I be afraid?" (Ps. 27:1 KJV).


We all know something about the Bible. So much of what we know is superficial. Just fun facts or trivia. But to many people, the Bible holds precious healing balm. It possesses a power to speak healing and truth. It's a source of comfort.

What God taught me early on regarding my health is still carrying me through the times when I can tell I won't be having one of my better days. I still draw strength and comfort from the Scriptures and meditation with God.

I'm thankful for physicians on earth. I'm even more so for the Great Physician, the one who is the author of the Word, who never requires that I schedule an appointment to visit with him.

"God is our refuge and strength, a very present help in trouble" (Ps. 46:1 ESV).

# CHAPTER 6

# A GOOD BOOK

*As for God, his way is perfect: / The Lord's word is flawless; /
he shields all who take refuge in him.*

—PSALM 18:30

*Let me live according to those holy rules which thou hast this day
prescribed in thy holy word; make me to know what is acceptable
in thy holy word; make me to know what is acceptable in thy sight,
and therin to delight, open the eyes of my understanding, and help
me thouroughly to examine myself according to my knowledge, faith,
and repentance, increase my faith, and direct me to the true object
Jesus Christ, the way, the truth, and the life.*

—GEORGE WASHINGTON'S PRAYER JOURNAL[1]

*Christ's heroism prized truth. . . . Jesus made love the supreme
value of the Kingdom of God.*

—VISHAL MANGALWADI, *THE BOOK
THAT MADE YOUR WORLD*

M any consider Abraham Lincoln our nation's finest president. He's certainly one of my favorites. In a speech he gave in Cincinnati, Ohio, on September 17, 1859, he said, "The good old maxims of the Bible are applicable, and truly applicable to human affairs, and in this as in other things, we may say here that he who is not for us is against us; he who gathereth not with us scattereth."[2]

Isn't it interesting that so many American leaders relied on the wisdom and ethics of the Bible? Not because they necessarily espoused the faith found in the Bible but because they acknowledged the wisdom that comes from its pages.

Every society is built on an ethic, or worldview. That ethic helps determine the rules that govern a society. There are simple rules we make that help keep order. For instance, when a citizen from London, England, moves to the United States, he has to learn to drive on the right side of the road. It doesn't matter that he has always driven on the left side. He must abide by the rule in order to keep the roads safe and free from chaos.

Just as a society must establish simple rules, like what side of the road to drive on, it also establishes cultural norms through other, more nuanced laws. What will help a society make these rules? Morality comes into play here. Rulers seek wisdom and knowledge to inform their decisions, their laws.

So societies must decide what worldview they will live by. Whose worldview will govern? Whether we admit it or not, every person and every society operates from a particular worldview. Some people describe a worldview as a lens through which you see the world.

As a society becomes more pluralistic, tensions between worldviews will arise. As a society, we must learn to live within these tensions. But what happens when one worldview is in conflict with another— when one worldview sees as right that which another worldview sees as wrong?

Are women of equal value as men? Do individuals have the right to hold their own opinions and to express them? Do citizens have the right to own property? These are all examples of basic tenets of a worldview.

My (Steve) first overseas business trip was in 1988. On the trip, we went to Hong Kong, China, Taiwan, and the Philippines. From Hong Kong, we took a train up through Shenzhen to Guangzhou, China. I remember looking out the window of the train at the countryside. Much of the trip, I saw farmland mile after mile. One picture that has always stuck in my mind is seeing a Chinese farmer all alone working a rice field. I thought, that person would never know anything but planting and harvesting rice. Their whole life, day in and day out, would be spent planting, harvesting, planting, harvesting.

I made that trip for more than twenty years, and over those years the landscape changed. All along the trip, I started seeing factories, offices, restaurants, homes—all gradually coming out of the ground. What I had thought would be the inevitable future of these farmers turned out to be wrong. If young enough, they had the opportunity to utilize their hidden ability. Was there a talent for construction, a mind for engineering, the creative propensity of a chef, artist, or interior designer? Such an ability would never have been utilized without the economic development I was witnessing.

How did this happen?

How did a nation see such development in such a short period of time?

I came up with two answers. First, America opened trade with China (1972), and second, China violated its own communistic principle and embraced a biblical principle: transferring property rights from the state to the individual.

Theologian Wayne Grudem reminds us that the Bible "assumes and enforces a system in which *property belongs to individuals*, not to the government or to a society as a whole." He points to, among other references, the Ten Commandments—such as the eighth commandment, "You shall not steal" (Ex. 20:15)—as implying this principle. "The assumption of private ownership of property," writes Grudem, "found in this fundamental moral code of the Bible, puts the Bible in direct opposition to the communist system advocated by Karl Marx. It was Karl Marx himself who said: 'The theory of the Communists may be summed up in the single sentence: abolition of private property.'"[3]

So as China developed and expanded special economic zones, the Chinese people received more incentives to produce, allowing for growth individually and economically. My observation? When a society employs biblical principles in establishing its rules, this is good for the society.

## You Can't Argue with a Good Thing

The Bible is a book for all, with a message for all, describing a set of principles of living for all.

Growing up, I knew my parents had a love for the Bible. Like Lincoln, my parents believed the maxims and principles of the Bible to be applicable for everyday life.

What I remember from the early days is the hard work. My dad worked hard at his day job, managing a general merchandise store, then came home to work on a new manufacturing start-up. My mom assembled picture frames, and my brother and I were part of the efforts too.

It was a family affair. A humble beginning.

I also remember the early money. Dad paid us for helping. Nothing significant, but enough for a young man to remember. He paid us seven cents for every frame we glued. It was just enough for a young boy to have some bubble gum money.

Mom and Dad always made sure we gave 10 percent to the church. That's just the way it was. I grew up viewing money through the lens of generosity.

But where did that lens come from? Why did Dad insist on this? It was a principle that came from the Bible.

It was the Bible that formed the ethic for our family and our business. An ethic is a set of moral principles. We all have them. It's just a question of what forms them. For us, it was the Bible. The first statement in our family business says that we operate our business according to biblical principles. Not that we have ever fully done that, but that is what we strive to do.

Have you heard of the term Judeo-Christian ethic? Today this phrase is sometimes met with political derision. But we forget that it was Friedrich Nietzsche, an influential German philosopher known for his disbelief in God, who first used it; he coined it. Later, Dwight D. Eisenhower referred to our country's Judeo-Christian ethic when he said, "Our sense of government has no sense unless it is founded in a deeply religious faith, and I don't care what it is. With us of course it is the Judeo-Christian concept, but it must be a religion that all men are created equal."[4]

Judeo-Christian ethic simply means a set of life-governing principles based on principles found in Judaism and Christianity. And we find those principles in the Bible. They are principles that have proven beneficial in governance and in family life. You don't have to adhere to a certain faith to enjoy the benefits of a Judeo-Christian ethic.

You can be a Hindu, a Muslim, an atheist, or even a communist and still benefit from the Bible's way to live.

Today there are many voices that will argue that the Bible is not good. In response to one of our holiday ads, a writer had this to say: "Christianity and its failure of reality-testing brought about the fall of the Roman Empire. It may bring the fall of world civilization as well." Wow, the fall of world civilization! Will the Bible really contribute to the fall of world civilization? There are many books that oppose the Bible and contribute to beliefs like this.

One such book, titled *God Is Not Great*, was written by Christopher Hitchens, an atheist. Notice its subtitle: "How Religion Poisons Everything." He and others have argued the dangers of religion. Now, to be truthful, there are many arguments that can be made against religion, as there have been many atrocities committed throughout history in the name of religion. The question that has to be asked is, were the atrocities committed following the tenets of the religion, or were they in violation of the tenets?

It's our belief you should not blame the Bible for man's misuse of it.

For example, there was a man named Jim Jones who took a group of people down to Guyana. In the fall of 1978, he told them to drink a poisonous mix of Kool-Aid and cyanide because the "church" he founded, which had turned cultic, was on the verge of being exposed. What an atrocity.

Hitler utilized messianic images, images of redemption, and other motifs of the Bible if it served his twisted purposes.

But don't blame the Bible for man's misuse of it.

There are many who have been hurt by those who have been looked up to as a faith leader. Faith leaders are imperfect people, just like the rest of us, and sometimes they make wrong choices. We've often said God has no option but to use imperfect people. That's all he's got. Every pastor is imperfect, every boss is imperfect, every spouse is imperfect, and every parent is imperfect. Man's imperfections don't make the book bad.

The Bible is honest with its heroes. It exposes their faults and failures, which only points out another truth the Bible teaches: no one is good. The only man the Bible claims to be good is Jesus.

So while there are many examples of people not "walking the walk," as the cliché goes, what we should ask ourselves is, what does the Bible teach about how we should act? Now, that's a big question, and there are many who spend their life studying that very thing. Is there a way to sum up what the Bible teaches? Can we find a simple answer to this question?

Yes. Just look at what Jesus says in Matthew:

> When the Pharisees heard that [Jesus] had silenced the Sadducees, they gathered together. And one of them, a lawyer, asked him a question to test him. "Teacher, which is the great commandment in the Law?" And he said to him, "You shall love the Lord your God with all your heart and with all your soul and with all your mind. This is the great and first commandment. And a second is like it: You shall love your neighbor as yourself. On these two commandments depend all the Law and the Prophets."
>
> —MATTHEW 22:34–40 ESV

Jesus claims that all of the Law and the Prophets are understood by loving God and loving others. When you take a look at the Ten Commandments, one of the most well-known portions of the Bible, you can divide them up between these two commands. The first four concern our love for God, and the final six concern our love for others.

A third portion of Scripture we could look at is what is referred to as the "love chapter." This is the thirteenth chapter of 1 Corinthians. It tells us what love looks like. It says, "Love is patient and kind; love does not envy or boast; it is not arrogant or rude. It does not insist on its own way; it is not irritable or resentful; it does not rejoice at wrongdoing, but rejoices with the truth. Love bears all things, believes all things, hopes all things, endures all things" (1 Cor. 13:4–7 ESV).

If we all lived according to this definition of love toward God and others, the world would be a much better place. Now, we are also told that those whom God loves he disciplines. It can be easy to view the idea of love today as this warm, fuzzy notion that serves us individually.

But the Bible teaches a different kind of love. Not a wimpy notion, full of pure emotion. Love possesses a tough side too. It makes a commitment to persevere. While love can be tough, it never loses its grace in how we treat each other.

I was born into a family that has tried to live according to the teachings of the Bible, I work for a company whose goal is to operate according to its principles, and I live in a country that was founded with its influence. None are without fault, but each has been blessed by its efforts to follow the Bible's direction.

These are big ideas. Love God. Love people. Persevere in love. And they are good ideas. I wholeheartedly disagree with anybody who would argue that the Bible is not good!

CHAPTER 7

# A MOST DANGEROUS BOOK

*You make your saving help my shield, / and your right hand sustains me; / your help has made me great. / You provide a broad path for my feet, / so that my ankles do not give way.*

—PSALM 18:35–36

*Anything more than scripture is too much. This may seem obvious, but it is something we often ignore. It is a confusion that has created recurring tension through the history of missions. And it creates tension still today when we can't resist including a few amendments to the gospel of grace.*

—M. R. THOMAS, *THE TURNING POINT*

*He is no fool who gives what he cannot keep to gain that which he cannot lose.*

—JIM ELLIOT

In the winter of 1531, Henry VIII was looking for help. He wanted to find articulate and passionate writers and thinkers to help him break the yoke that the pope continued to have on England. One of his advisors gave him a book by a "zealot" who laid out some striking ideas against "the accursed power of the pope." So Henry sent Stephen Vaughan to find the book's author: William Tyndale.

Tyndale converted to Protestantism during his time studying at Oxford. Historians say he was "full of imagination and eloquence, active and ready to endure fatigue" and dangerous in the fulfillment of his mission. His mission? To translate the Bible into the English language. Just the kind of man King Henry was looking for.

But Tyndale was a ghost. He wrote in seclusion, and the most anyone could find on his whereabouts were rumors. Even so, Vaughan heard that he was in Antwerp, Belgium, so he traveled to Belgium to find him. For three months Vaughan remained in Antwerp, looking for Tyndale. But he found nothing.

Then one day (April 17, 1531), as he was copying one of Tyndale's manuscripts to send to Henry, he heard a knock on his door.

"Someone, who calls himself a friend of yours, desires very much to speak with you," said the stranger, "and begs you to follow me."

"Who is this friend? Where is he?" asked Vaughan.

"I do not know him," replied the messenger, "but come along, and you will see for yourself."

It was risky. Vaughan didn't know who this messenger was, and he certainly had no clue who the "friend" was who so desperately wanted to see him. But his curiosity got the better of him, so he agreed to follow the messenger. They wound their way out of Antwerp to a lonely field, where the Scheldt River flowed on one side. Vaughan continued to walk across the field, when he saw a man appear. He looked noble.

"Do you recognize me?" he asked Vaughan.

"I cannot call to mind your features," answered Vaughan.

"My name is Tyndale."[1]

And so it was in a lonely field that Henry's messenger found the invisible Tyndale. But this was just the dramatic beginning to a most dramatic tale of intrigue and danger. Tyndale continued his work on translation but did not endear himself to Henry VIII. He was a bit too edgy for the king. For though Henry sought to break from the pope, he also viewed Tyndale as a visionary whose work in translation was full of lies and sedition.

A 1553 copy of Tyndale's New Testament. Tyndale printed the first English translation of the New Testament in 1526 (Green Collection).

They were at an impasse. Henry wanted to break from Rome, but Tyndale wanted a Bible translation for the everyman.

Tyndale had already translated the New Testament in 1525 but was working hard on the Old Testament. He kept at it even when he was imprisoned in 1535. His conviction came a year later. He was found guilty of heresy and was executed by strangulation; then his dead body was burned at the stake. His friend Vaughan tried to save his body from the burning stake but failed.

Tyndale knew the dangers involved in translating a book that, up to that point, had been used only by the clergy because it was written in Latin, Greek, and Hebrew. Like other Reformers, Tyndale counted the cost and gave his life to the cause of Bible translation.

## Out-of-the-Box Principles

The Bible is everywhere.

The Bible is useful.

The Bible is dangerous.

As Tyndale could have attested, the Bible is more than a book. It contains maxims and principles. World leaders have used it for guidance. And plenty of ordinary men and women, like us, have also used it for guidance and as a source of hope and comfort.

But what we don't always talk about is how dangerous this book is. We take it for granted too often. We forget that people, like William Tyndale, sacrificed their lives so that one day every person with a smartphone or computer could download this great book. Risk is a big part of its story, but it's also part of ours.

Earlier we told you a story about some of our financial troubles related to having two houses in the early years of our marriage. It was during those hard financial times we made a decision that wasn't popular with many of our friends. We decided then and there to pursue a life in which we lived debt free. It was a risk we took when we, in faith, agreed to live by one of the Bible's principles regarding debt.

Some may read our get-out-of-debt story and say, "Well, that's not really that dangerous." And we'd agree. We didn't live with a constant threat on our lives, but although our debt-free story might lack real-world danger, it was nevertheless a risky proposition for us. We're like anyone else. We enjoy the comforts of modern society.

For us, getting out of debt was a matter of commitment. Were we going to live our lives according to the principles of this book or not? We believe that one of the dangers of following this book is the testing we face to determine our commitment to follow its principles.

We attended a conference that taught biblical concepts regarding stewardship. For the first time in our lives, we learned that the Bible teaches to owe man nothing.

In the New Testament book of Romans, for example, the apostle Paul says, "Pay to all what is owed to them: taxes to whom taxes are owed, revenue to whom revenue is owed, respect to whom respect is owed, honor to whom honor is owed. Owe no one anything, except to love each other, for the one who loves another has fulfilled the law" (Rom. 13:7–8 ESV). Again, in the Old Testament book of Proverbs, the writer reminds us that "the borrower is the slave of the lender" (Prov. 22:7 ESV).

So we made a decision to get out of debt. It was a tough decision. I mentioned previously that just before we married, Steve purchased a house from his brother as an investment property. We never would have guessed that the tenants would skip town owing several months of rent. The house became a drain on our finances, especially in light of the oil bust in Oklahoma at the time. We committed to getting rid of that burden and living debt free.

We had an empty rental house, and Steve had just moved into a new house before we were married. The value of all houses in the market had gone down. Within a year, we were able to sell off the rental house, which stopped the negative spiral on our finances. That was a relief, but when it came time for us to list the home we were living in, that was a different level of commitment.

We did not know what we would do when the house sold; we would just take it one day at a time, trusting God in the risk we were taking. We listed our home so we could pay off the debt that was owed.

The problem was, after having the house on the market for several months, we realized it would not sell for enough to pay off the mortgage. If we sold the home for what we could get out of it, we would still be in debt. We wanted God's best, but we felt God was saying no. Maybe he was telling us we had gotten ourselves into this situation, and he wanted to know if we were really committed to his best. So we took the house off the market and determined to pay off the house the best we could, as quickly as we could.

We committed to pay any extra we had to the mortgage company. A little here, a little there, any extra from Steve's annual bonus check, was sent to go straight toward the principal. We buckled down on our budget and committed to live within our means. As the years went on and God saw our commitment, the day came when we were able to pay off our mortgage. It was such a day of freedom—no more being a slave to the lender!

It was scary for us as newlyweds. When you're young and married and everyone around you is living beyond their means, it's tough to say, "No, we're going to do what we can to live by the principles set before us in this book." We took the risk and found reward.

This book poses many challenges to people. Living by faith, when our society preaches self-reliance. Sacrificing for others, when our society says look out for number one. Leaving the prospects of a good-paying job and the security it brings to live in a foreign country as a missionary. These are not particularly dangerous, though they do all carry some element of risk. And yet there are some who do give up everything, even their lives, to ensure all people hear about this book.

## Real Danger

It was January 2, 1956. Jim Elliot and his missionary friends finally had made contact with the previously unreached, and very violent, Waorani people on a sandbar in the remote jungles of Ecuador. They planned this meeting over a three-year span. During that period, their missionary work focused on the Quichua tribe, and many converted to Christianity.

But the Waorani people were different. They had killed many of the Quichua people. Yet their history did not deter the intentions of these missionaries. The missionaries landed one by one on the sandbar and waited as Nick Saint flew overhead and invited the Waorani to the beach. A Waorani man and two women appeared later on the beach. The initial meetings with the three tribespeople seemed to go well. The missionaries sat with them. They tried to communicate with them by drawing in the sand and using a model of the bush plane they flew. They tried to show friendship and asked them, in their limited knowledge of their language, to invite more people from their tribe to the beach.

They waited for two days for them to return.

Finally, two Waorani women walked out of the jungle. Excited, Jim Elliot and Pete Fleming waded across the water to greet them. But then they heard a scream behind them. It was a group of Waorani warriors standing with spears raised. Though Jim had a gun on him, the group of five missionaries promised each other they would not kill a Waorani person if they had not yet heard about Jesus Christ. In moments, the warriors released their spears and killed all five of the American missionaries: Jim Elliot, Nate Saint, Peter Fleming, Ed McCully, and Roger Youderian.

It turned into national news in America. *Life* magazine reported the tragedy.

In the New Testament book of Matthew, one of the four gospel accounts, Jesus leaves his disciples with one final charge. It's an intense scene. Jesus stands before his friends as a resurrected man, and in moments he will ascend to heaven. Just before he leaves, he says, "Go therefore and make disciples of all nations, baptizing them in the name of the Father and of the Son and of the Holy Spirit, teaching them to observe all that I have commanded you. And behold, I am with you always, to the end of the age" (Matt. 28:19–20 ESV).

This final charge Jesus gave his disciples is commonly referred to as the Great Commission. Jesus commissioned all of his followers, from that point to the present age, to carry his message of forgiveness of sins and eternal life to the world.

Jim Elliot and his team of missionaries were following Jesus' instructions. And they paid the ultimate price.

Following the principles of this book requires commitment, and sometimes it is risky. The cost for some may be losing their relationships with friends or family, their job, their education, their security— and there are people who have lost their lives. So often in life, the hardest things we go through bring the greatest rewards.

The bottom line looks like this: When we follow the principles found in the Bible, our lives will look different. Maybe even countercultural. And that's okay. As Jim Elliot said, "He is no fool who gives what he cannot keep to gain that which he cannot lose."

Jim and his team did not die in vain. They paid the ultimate price, but their martyrdom inspired a whole generation of missionaries to follow in their footsteps. Now even the Waorani people, including the ones who speared Jim, Nate, Pete, Roger, and Ed to death, are missionaries to others.

Many of them began to live by the principles set forth in the Bible. Their tribe was completely changed, which was documented by Clayton and Carole Robarchek, anthropologists who studied them later. In their book *Waorani: Contexts of Violence and War,* they point out that "during the past century, more than 60 percent of Waorani deaths have been the result of homicide, making this the most violent society known to anthropology."[2]

They go on to say, "Regardless of what else went on, however, there was one constant refrain: because they heard/believed/understood/obeyed the Word of God, they no longer allowed themselves to become angry and therefore they no longer speared. The commitment to this nonviolent way of life distinguished them from other Waorani who did not believe, and ensured a good and a peaceful life for them all."[3]

# PART 3

# COLLECTING SECRETS

קְרָא אֵלַי

*Call to me and I will answer you and tell you great and unsearchable things you do not know.*

—JEREMIAH 33:3

*God can be loved only when He is known. That's why the story of the Bible is the story of God revealing Himself in order to draw to Himself obedient worship, or glory, from the nations. With God's passionate love at the core, the Bible is truly the story of His glory.*

—STEVEN C. HAWTHORNE,
*THE STORY OF HIS GLORY*

CHAPTER 8

# THE MUSEUM OF
# THE BIBLE

*"If you hold to my teaching, you are really my disciples. Then you
will know the truth, and the truth will set you free."*

—JOHN 8:31–32

*It was staggering to me how modern archaeology could finally
unlock the significance of a statement in which Jesus boldly asserted
nearly two thousand years ago that he was indeed the anointed
one of God.*

—LEE STROBEL, *THE CASE FOR CHRIST*

*Once you have renounced everything, really everything, then any
bold enterprise becomes the simplest and most natural thing in
the world.*

—ANGELO RONCALLI[1]

They couldn't believe their ears. What was she thinking? Could it actually be true?

The words sank in for a moment; then the two men ran out of the room. Hearts pounding. Minds racing.

Scenarios swirled through their brains. Maybe she visited the wrong one. Maybe she was just scared.

But what if it was true? Then what? What if everything they'd discussed over all those years was true! And now they were running into that truth.

Out of breath, the surlier man stopped short of the destination, huffing and puffing. His friend outran him and arrived first at the structure. He did not go in. Instead he stood in the doorway and looked inside.

It was dusty and dark. He waited for his eyes to adjust. The place smelled stale and cold but strangely new.

His eyes finally adjusted, he scanned the room. He couldn't believe what he saw.

The surly man pushed through the opening.

"Well," he said, "what is it? Is it—"

He didn't finish his question. His eyes answered for him. The outside light permeated the dark room, his eyes adjusted, and he let out a shout of alarm and joy.

His friend now entered the room. The surly man, named Peter, turned and grabbed him by the shoulder. "John, it's true. It's really true. He rose from the dead!"

The two men walked back along the dirt road to the house where the rest of their friends waited. They could barely contain their emotion during their return. But they knew they must be careful. If the temple guard discovered what they had discovered, they'd suspect foul play.

They entered the house.

"John, is it true? What did you see?"

"It is true," Peter said, interrupting. "The tomb is empty."

"Peter, what do we do?" another asked.

"We pray."

## A Story of Discovery

When was the last time you discovered something for the first time? Maybe it was a fact or figure you spent so much time researching and finally found? Maybe it was something about a friend or loved one—your family history, perhaps?

Discovery invigorates us. It presents us with evidence of something, a truth. When we discover, we in essence pull back the veil and reveal the truth of something. When Einstein discovered the law of relativity, he pulled back the veil on a truth. When those two sisters discovered that ancient manuscript in Saint Catherine's Monastery, they pulled back the veil on a part of world history.

The story above describes what it might have been like for the disciples of Jesus when they discovered the empty tomb. Of course, we don't know whether Peter was a burly, weathered Galilean man or what John looked like. We thought we'd add some more descriptive elements to the story to help our imaginations see the men distinctly.

If the discovery is true, it would be the greatest discovery ever made. As C. S. Lewis said, "Christianity, if false, is of no importance, and if true, of infinite importance. The only thing it cannot be is moderately important."[2]

In John's gospel account, we first find the tomb visited by Mary Magdalene, another of Jesus' disciples. It was Mary who discovered that the stone they rolled in front of the tomb had been moved. Surprised and alarmed, Mary ran back to the other disciples to tell them the news: "They have taken the Lord's body out of the tomb, and we don't know where they have put him!" (John 20:2 NLT).

When John and Peter heard the news, they ran to the tomb. John was one of Jesus' closest friends and disciples. Peter was also part of Jesus' inner circle. John reached the tomb first. He stooped and looked in and saw the linen that formerly wrapped Jesus' body. But he did not go in. Peter, on the other hand, rushed past John and into the tomb. They both saw the place where Jesus should have been lying dead, wrapped in linen.

But all they found was the linen wrappings. Jesus had spoken to them about this moment. But until now, they had not understood what he meant. Peter and John left the tomb to rejoin the other disciples. But Mary Magdalene, who had followed them back to the tomb, stayed.

She stooped into the opening, and she too discovered an empty tomb. Just linen wrappings. But apparently, she was still not convinced of the reality before her eyes. She walked out of the tomb and stood crying, thinking thieves broke in and took the body of Jesus.

What took place next Eugene Peterson paraphrases in *The Message* this way:

Mary stood outside the tomb weeping. As she wept, she knelt to look into the tomb and saw two angels sitting there, dressed in white, one at the head, the other at the foot of where Jesus' body had been laid. They said to her, "Woman, why do you weep?"

"They took my Master," she said, "and I don't know where they put him." After she said this, she turned away and saw Jesus standing there. But she didn't recognize him.

Jesus spoke to her, "Woman, why do you weep? Who are you looking for?"

She, thinking that he was the gardener, said, "Mister, if you took him, tell me where you put him so I can care for him."

Jesus said, "Mary."

Turning to face him, she said in Hebrew, *"Rabboni!"* meaning "Teacher!"

Jesus said, "Don't cling to me, for I have not yet ascended to the Father. Go to my brothers and tell them, 'I ascend to my Father and your Father, my God and your God.'"

Mary Magdalene went, telling the news to the disciples: "I saw the Master!" And she told them everything he said to her.

—JOHN 20:11–18 MSG

John fills his account of this scene with excitement, wonder, and epiphany. Mary's response to Jesus? Priceless. Her eyes opened. The veil pulled back. If true, it would be the discovery of all ages.

Most scholars, in varying degrees, agree that a man named Jesus of Nazareth, a great teacher, walked this earth.

The story of Jesus' death combines both incredibly vivid narrative and history at the same time. Again, most scholars will acquiesce to the notion of Jesus dying by Roman crucifixion. And if you want to really dive deep into the story, check out John's account of the last week of Jesus' life.

John's gospel account reads much differently than the other gospels. And a majority of his book looks closely at what many now refer to as "the passion of Jesus," which just means the week leading up to and culminating in Jesus' crucifixion.

But what other texts or artifacts exist that pull back the veil on the world in which Jesus lived, worked, and engaged in his ministry endeavors? What other discoveries have been made?

## Pulling Back the Veil on Jesus' World

In recent years, archaeological discoveries focusing on the area where Jesus lived have provided us with new glimpses into Jesus' world. For example, archaeologists recently discovered a synagogue in the area thought to be the hometown of Mary Magdalene, one of Jesus' most devoted followers. The find revealed benches erected against the walls, a mosaic floor, and "a mysterious stone block, the size of a toy chest, unlike anything anyone had seen before."[3]

The mysterious stone is referred to as the Magdala Stone, and it represents one of the most significant archaeological finds in recent decades. Carved into the stone are "a seven-branched menorah, a chariot of fire and a hoard of symbols associated with the most hallowed precincts of the Jerusalem temple."[4] Scholars continue to analyze the stone but brim with excitement because of the potential insight the stone can give to help us understand this area called Galilee and why it was the perfect place to launch a world religion.

It's an exciting find that helps us see into that ancient world. There's still much work to be done in the field of New Testament archaeology, but it seems the pieces to the story-puzzle continue to shed light on the Bible itself.

Discovery begins with willingness. A willingness to explore, to suspend belief or disbelief and follow where the evidence leads. Most people believe Jesus walked the earth. Most even believe he endured the humiliating Roman crucifixion, an execution style reserved for the lowliest of people. These two events are recorded in the Bible.

We don't use the Bible primarily for history or archaeology, though we do find helpful information in it with regard to these fields. Likewise, we have found so much in these two fields that continue to support the Bible.

Think about the crucifixion, for example. It's a fact that the Romans utilized this type of execution.[5] In 1968, archaeologists discovered a first-century tomb in Jerusalem in which "a skeletal heel nailed to a board by an iron spike was found in an ossuary, or bone box."[6] This evidence proves to us that the Romans crucified people in the way Jesus is said to have been crucified.

But consider the words of the Old Testament prophet Isaiah.

The Bible indicates Isaiah prophesied more than seven hundred years before the time of Jesus.

And in the now-famous passage of Isaiah 53, we read of the way in which Jesus will be killed: "He was pierced for our transgressions . . . crushed for our iniquities . . . and by his wounds we are healed" (Isa. 53:5).

We read that he will be among criminals when he dies: "[He] was numbered with the transgressors" (Isa. 53:12).

In verse 7, Isaiah says, "He was oppressed and afflicted, yet he did not open his mouth." In the gospel accounts found in the New Testament, we see Jesus standing before Pilate and Herod Antipas, silent, refusing to speak out for himself (John 19:8–10; Luke 23:8–9).

Jesus was buried in the tomb of a rich man (John 19:38–42), an odd practice for someone who was crucified, but not unheard of. Isaiah says, "They made his grave with the wicked and with a rich man in his death" (Isa. 53:9 ESV).

Wouldn't it be great if a place existed that encouraged exploration and discovery? A museum, perhaps?

## A Vision for What Could Be

While we never pictured ourselves as collectors of ancient biblical artifacts, we were fortunate that we could proceed to launch the building of a space in Washington, D.C., that will allow everyone to understand how vital these artifacts are to our lives as human beings. We wanted to tell the story of the Bible, the story we shared above. It's our heart's desire to do it in a way that invites people from all walks of life and all faith traditions to come and explore.

We eased into the idea of the museum, becoming more of a partner in the project. We took on more responsibility, because we owned the artifacts and we desired a home for these treasures. At the time, the people we'd initially started working with on the artifact collection wanted to open a museum in Dallas, Texas. Several buildings were looked at, but none of them met our needs. As the collection grew, we considered locations in the top-ten metro areas in the United States.

Two other cities stood out to me: New York City and Washington, D.C. We engaged a gentleman to scout out all three cities for a potential site. That's when we decided we should find out whether anyone else thought our dream was a good idea. The question was, if we build it, will they come? We commissioned a nationwide survey asking one thousand Americans across the country a hundred questions by phone.

The response was overwhelming.

Over 80 percent of those surveyed agreed it was a good idea. The surveyor came in to report his findings, and his comment was that if you can get 75 percent of Americans to agree on anything, then it will be successful. When he saw that it was 80 percent positive, he knew we had an idea that would work.

But a winning idea doesn't guarantee success. A concept for a new restaurant may be a good idea. But restaurants get started and go out of business all the time. We knew we'd have to build a museum with a high standard of excellence.

We also found out from the surveys that the museum would be best attended in Washington, D.C.; New York City came in second, and Dallas was third. We decided we would focus our efforts on D.C. It just made sense, because D.C. is the home to so many world-class museums in our country, making the chance of success so much greater. With our Hobby Lobby stores, we found that we always do best when we are located with other big-box stores, so being with other museums in D.C. was logical.

We also learned that as many as 20 percent of visitors to D.C. were international. Therefore we knew that the Bible's story would have worldwide exposure. After looking at many sites all over D.C., we were told that the Washington Design Center, a building located at 4th and D Street S.W., was going on the market. We looked at it and decided to make an offer. In 2012, we acquired the building. We now had a home, and now the work of making the dream come alive would begin.

For the next two years, we planned, strategized, and designed a Bible museum. We engaged the best people in their fields to help us make sure what we did was done with excellence. Then, in October of 2014, we held our first dinner to bring awareness to the project. People from all over the country came. Over the next two years, we held 160 such dinners, with many more to come. The buzz was officially, well, "buzzing."

Early on, we decided to look at the Bible in three different ways: its *history*, its *narrative*, and its *impact*. In the museum, we dedicate a floor to each of these, and we developed curriculum with these three aspects in mind.

The history floor explores the Bible's history. What has archaeology told us about what the Bible says? What manuscript evidence exists for the Bible? Then we move on to the print and digital age of the Bible's history.

Also on the history floor, we look into the efforts to finalize the translation of the Bible into every language in the world. It's a historic effort. Never in the history of the world has a book been translated into every language. There's not even a close second, and that effort is highlighted on this floor.

For the narrative floor, we keep in mind the person who doesn't know the Bible's story. It is a high-level look at *this story*. Wanting to be respectful of our Jewish guests, we tell the story in three parts. First, we tell the story of the Hebrew text in a timed walk-through. Second, we show the town in which Jesus grew up. It's called "The World of Jesus of Nazareth." Finally, we tell the New Testament story in a theater setting.

The impact floor shows how the Bible speaks into and has impacted every area of life. I am convinced that the average person has no idea of the degree to which the Bible has affected his or her life. From the money we exchange on a daily basis to the concepts and principles that shaped our early government documents, our economy, the medical field, education, art, music, literature, and on and on—the Bible's impact reaches far and wide.

Our love for this book translated into a desire to have the world understand it at a level never seen before. And we thought that if we were going to build a museum for the Bible, it needed to be a world-class facility unlike anything people had ever experienced.

## The Unifying Power of the Bible

We grew up in a home where the Bible was central. Our love for it grew from an early age. For us, to see these artifacts that represent the foundation of what we've always believed is inspiring. We truly believe the museum will encourage people of all walks of life, of all faith traditions.

It will do different things for different people.

Anyone who possesses a sense of history will realize the amazing cost so many people like William Tyndale paid to translate this book for everyone to read.

You're a skeptic? That's great. It will arouse your curiosity. It will make you wonder why you never heard some of the amazing facts about the Bible before.

We believe the Bible can stand on its own. We're not creating a place to proselytize. We feel our job is to share the Bible's story in an engaging way. We want people to walk through the museum and leave inspired to dig deeper, and be intrigued by the book itself.

Our goal? To help people understand this amazing book a little better.

We grew up in a small denominational church. As we grew in our knowledge of the Bible, we found differences in beliefs within our church, which led us to attend another church. It was also during this time that we were homeschooling our kids. I (Steve) remember going to our homeschool group meetings and developing new friendships. What I also remember was that we had a lot in common with those families even though we attended a variety of different churches. With our new church, we found that we had differences with its teachings. These experiences taught me that no matter the church, no matter the denomination, no matter the background, we could always find differences with what we believed. On the other hand, the Bible was our unifying factor. And if we were able to admit that none of us had it all figured out, we could have a fair exchange of ideas yet still be supportive of each other in our endeavors to follow the teachings outlined in the Bible.

As we've traveled the country, speaking with people about this great project, we've had the opportunity to talk to people with varying faith traditions. These conversations thrill us. We've discovered a synergy with others around the museum. Some of the walls built up over misconceptions have disintegrated.

People from all walks of life will look at this museum and see it as something good and interesting. How amazing! We find this notion of commonality so important, especially considering the hard lines of division in our country and our world.

It makes me think of our exhibit we had in Cuba. Our first international exhibit was at the Vatican in 2012. It had gone so well that we were asked to come back the next year. We asked if we could consider returning in 2014. While we were there in 2012, the pope at the time, Pope Benedict, made a historic trip to Cuba, which was still a closed country then. We were told by several people that he mentioned our exhibit and that maybe the exhibit could make its way to Cuba.

We decided to investigate the possibility, and after a lot of work, the doors began to open. In 2014, we had our first exhibit at the National Cathedral in Havana, Cuba, with approximately thirty thousand people visiting the exhibit over a thirty-day period. On opening night, a stage was set up outside the cathedral. The entire area was filled with chairs, and there was standing room only. There were even people on their balconies surrounding the town square. On the stage, the Cubans put on a show telling the Bible's story from Genesis to Revelation. The performance ended with a standing ovation to the "Hallelujah Chorus."

We later learned that the production was put on by both the Catholic and Protestant churches working together. Amazingly, this one exhibit about the Bible required the American government's approval and the Cuban government's approval, and it was the Catholic and Protestant churches coming together to make it happen. It was just an indication of the unity that the book made possible.

If we had clung to the narrow Protestant perspective we'd had growing up, this would not be the case. Things have changed in this manner for us. Over the years, we've learned—and continue to learn—that people of various denominations and faith traditions have more things in common than we might think. They love their families and want the best for their kids. The ability of the museum to bring so many different people together has been incredible to watch.

The Bible creates a common bond between so many people, and we believe there is real power in celebrating this, while at the same time being honest and generous toward one another with regard to our differences. Differences are good. The question is, how are we going to respond to those differences? That's the key. But let's lay our differences aside, at least for the length of the museum tour, and celebrate this book we love.

# CHAPTER 9

# THE DEAD SEA AND THE FIRST SCRIPTURES

*When [a king] takes the throne of his kingdom, he is to write for himself on a scroll a copy of this law, taken from that of the Levitical priests. It is to be with him, and he is to read it all the days of his life so that he may learn to revere the LORD his God and follow carefully all the words of this law and these decrees.*

—DEUTERONOMY 17:18–19

*Understanding our civilization and understanding the Bible may be important reasons for reading the Old Testament, but perhaps the most important reason is that it is the Bible Jesus read.*

—PHILIP YANCEY, *THE BIBLE JESUS READ*

*One day—but there's no hurry—you may come to read the Bible. Nowhere else will you find so many stories about ancient times so vividly told.*

—E. H. GOMBRICH, *A LITTLE HISTORY OF THE WORLD*

t's an overwhelming sight. I got choked up, and wasn't expecting to."

That was the response of one of our friends after we showed him the collection of Torah scrolls in our museum warehouse.

"I expected to walk into a regular-sized room and see casings of scrolls. But then I walked in. It was like a warehouse inside of a warehouse. Massive shelves held the scrolls and went all the way to the ceiling. I didn't know how to respond. So I cried."

What is it about *seeing* these manuscripts that evokes such an emotional response?

"When you think about the history behind each one of those scrolls," he continued, "how each one represents the world of several scribes who lived so long ago, and they're preserved like that, just waiting to be seen. Well, it's moving."

## The Beginning of the Bible

The Torah scrolls represent the superb accuracy of the Jewish people. The Bible, as we know it today, stands on the shoulders of the Jewish people and their attention to detail and vigilance in copying the text of the Old Testament for millennia.

What is a Torah scroll?

A Torah scroll is a handwritten copy of the Torah. The word *Torah* means "the Law" or "instruction," and it is used to describe the first five books of our modern-day Bible: Genesis, Exodus, Leviticus, Numbers, Deuteronomy. Remember, books as we know them were not invented until the first century. Before books, then, we had scrolls.

Another name for the Torah is the word *Pentateuch*. It comes from a Greek term meaning "five-scroll work." One of the most famous scrolls is the Isaiah Scroll. It was found in the caves of Qumran in 1942 and is one of the longest ancient scrolls in existence today, measuring about twenty-four feet long. The most popular books or scrolls in ancient times were copied the most.

The Museum of the Bible owns one of the largest private collections of Torah scrolls, spanning more than seven hundred years of history, including Torahs that survived the Spanish Inquisition, scrolls confiscated by the Nazis during World War II, and others. The sheer number of Torah scrolls in existence today speaks to the popularity of these texts over time and, in our opinion, to the veracity of the message within the scrolls.

MOTB.SCR.003572

Miniature Torah Scroll with Green Belt and Mantle,
Russia, 19th century (Museum of the Bible).

So the Torah is important, even foundational to the rest of the Bible. The New Testament quotes Genesis thirty-four times, quotes the book of Exodus forty-four times, and makes seventy-two references to Abraham.

So you can see the interconnectedness of the Torah with the entirety of the Bible; it is cohesive with the rest of the Scriptures. But the Old Testament consists of more than the Torah, though that is its foundation.

The Jews refer to the Hebrew Scriptures as the Tanakh, from the word *Tanakh*, an acronym derived from the Hebrew letters Torah (T), Nevi'im (N), and Ketuvim (K). So the Torah makes up part of the threefold compilation of the Hebrew Scriptures: Torah (Pentateuch), Nevi'im (Prophets), and Ketuvim (Writings).

The division of the Tanakh looks like this:

| Pentateuch / Torah | The Twelve Prophets | Writings / Ketuvim |
|---|---|---|
| Genesis *(Beginning)* | Hosea | Psalms |
| Exodus | Joel | Proverbs |
| Leviticus | Amos | Job |
| Numbers | Obadiah | Song of Songs |
| Deuteronomy | Jonah | Ruth |
| | Micah | Lamentations |
| **Prophets / Nevi'im** | Nahum | Ecclesiastes |
| Joshua | Habakkuk | Esther |
| Judges | Zephaniah | Daniel |
| 1 & 2 Samuel | Haggai | Ezra |
| 1 & 2 Kings | Zechariah | Nehemiah |
| Isaiah | Malachi | 1 & 2 Chronicles |
| Jeremiah | | *(End)* |
| Ezekiel | | |

Jesus refers to several books from the Hebrew Scriptures, quoting from every book of the Pentateuch and most often from the books of Exodus, Isaiah, Deuteronomy, and Psalms (from the latter over eleven times). The apostle Paul, who wrote the majority of the New Testament, used the Hebrew Scriptures often, quoting them to support doctrinal issues and to lend authority to his arguments.[1]

Perhaps even more interesting is the fact that the final book of the Bible, Revelation, refers to the Hebrew Scriptures more than does any other New Testament book: more than 350 references.[2] And so we see how the Torah works like a foundation upon which the rest of the Hebrew Scriptures unfold. When looking at the Bible as a whole, we see that the Torah, Prophets, and Writings find further illumination in the New Testament writers and most notably in the teachings of Jesus.

So we see that the Hebrew Scriptures form the foundation of the Bible, but what's so special about this foundation that even Jesus himself would consistently go back to it?

## God Writes on Stones

When we begin taking the Bible apart piece by piece, we can see how the Torah acts like a hinge. The rest of the Bible opens up through it.

In Exodus (the second book of the Torah), God told Moses to write down the things God would tell him. God said, "I am the LORD your God, who brought you out of Egypt, out of the land of slavery. You shall have no other gods before me. You shall not make for yourself an image in the form of anything in heaven above or on the earth beneath or in the waters below. You shall not bow down to them or worship them" (Ex. 20:1–5).

The Bible claims these were the actual spoken words of God. The Israelites *heard* them and were terrified. But Moses comforted them, saying, "Do not be afraid. God has come to test you, so that the fear of God will be with you to keep you from sinning" (Ex. 20:20).

After Moses said this, God summoned him to the top of Mount Sinai, and we read the incredible story of God giving Moses the Ten

Commandments. God actually wrote his commandments on stone tablets. This was a common practice in the ancient Near East. When a king wanted something decreed, he would have it inscribed on stone tablets. After God gave Moses the commandments, he continued to talk to Moses, and Moses wrote their conversations down. Joshua then added to the writings, and then the prophets also added to them.

So from the Torah to the Prophets to the Writings, God speaks to humanity. This is the claim of the Hebrew Scriptures.

The importance of the Torah, and the writings of the Old Testament in general, fueled our desire to do what we could to preserve such significant artifacts for the museum. So we began accumulating Torah scrolls, as well as a small collection of Dead Sea Scroll fragments.

## Lost and Found: The Dead Sea Scrolls

In 1947, three young Ta'amireh Bedouin shepherds tended their flocks on the northwest side of the Dead Sea, an area known as Qumran. One of the young shepherds, Muhammed edh-Dhib, entertained himself by throwing rocks at the openings of some of the nearby caves that were situated along the face of the cliffs. One of the stones made its way into a small opening of a cave and made a shattering sound.

But they didn't immediately check out the cause of the sound. They went home. It wasn't until the next day that another one of the boys decided to explore the cave. When he did, he made one of the most incredible archaeological finds of the twentieth century.

He found ten clay jars. Stashed in one of the jars, he found three ancient manuscripts. More manuscripts were found in that same cave, but not in the jars.

But the story is not so cut-and-dried. In a later interview, Muhammed describes how he "lowered himself through the entrance hold and dropped into the cave" and saw "47 jars."[3] But the cave was dark inside. Luckily for Muhammed, he was smoking his pipe and carried matches. So he used the matches to illuminate the cave.[4]

Muhammed goes on to tell how he called for his five friends, and they worked their way through all forty-seven jars. Only one jar contained scrolls—five of them. Another jar contained a scroll, but when they picked it up, it broke into pieces. So to them it was worthless. And they tossed it outside the cave. Most likely it was lost forever.[5]

The five scrolls in the other jar were made of leather. The boys thought the leather "might be good for sandal straps, so they took them back to their tents."[6] The boys kept the scrolls for another three years in a bag in the corner of the tent. At one point, the kids in the tribe obtained one of the scrolls and used it as a toy until it broke into pieces and they threw it in the trash.[7]

Facsimile of "Persher Isaiah" (4Q162), an essay interpreting the prophecy of Isaiah according to the ideology of the Qumran sect (Hebrew). Details: Handwritten, ink on parchment. Place: Qumran, Israel / 1st century BC (National Christian Foundation).

NCF.FAC.000115.8

More controversy and conspiracy lingers around the actual discovery dates. For instance, the authorities at Saint Mark's Monastery, who made the find public, tried to conceal the actual date, claiming they'd kept the scrolls safe in their monastery for centuries.[8] Needless to say, the momentous find opened up the area to more exploration. Archaeologists discovered more caves and more manuscripts.

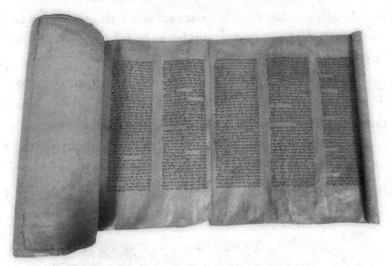

A Sephardic Torah scroll associated with the Jews predominantly from the Iberian Peninsula (Spain and Portugal) and North Africa (Museum of the Bible).
MOTB.SCR.003573

We know the scrolls found in that initial discovery by the Bedouin boys as the Dead Sea Scrolls. To date, the entirety of the discovered Dead Sea Scrolls amounts to nine hundred separate manuscripts in over twenty-five thousand pieces. Some scrolls, like the famed Isaiah Scroll, are almost completely intact. Others are only bits and pieces, deteriorated over time.

Archaeologists categorized the scrolls into seven different types of texts, ranging from biblical texts to mystical texts. Scholars continue to debate whether the community there at Qumran produced the scrolls or if many of them came from somewhere outside the community. The Dead Sea Scrolls remain one of the most significant discoveries in biblical archaeology and continue to add to the discussion surrounding the accuracy of what we have for the Old Testament.

## So What?

What significance do the Dead Sea Scrolls hold for us in our day-to-day lives and for our own exploration of the Bible?

Varying theories circulate with regard to the Qumran community who copied texts, archived them, and wrote new texts in the desert. But most would agree that this "select group of Essenes lived at the Qumran site from about 100–50 BC until AD 68 . . . and when moving to the desert, they took with them scrolls deriving from various places in Israel."

These scrolls pull back the veil from the world of Jewish literature and provide us with insight into the many genres we find in the Old Testament and extrabiblical literature of the time. We can see how the biblical text was transmitted over this time frame. And though variations occur in the text, our understanding of the text that we call our Old Testament continues to grow.

The Dead Sea Scrolls now give scholars "Hebrew manuscripts dated one thousand years earlier than the great Masoretic Text manuscripts, enabling them to check the fidelity of the Hebrew text." So how big is the discrepancy between texts? It's estimated that only a 5 percent variation exists, which are merely slips of the pen. And what of the other 95 percent? Word-for-word identity![9]

Take Isaiah 53, for example. There are 166 words in this chapter. Of those words, only 17 letters in the Isaiah B scroll differ from those in the Masoretic Text—which, you'll recall, is one thousand years

younger—and those variations do not greatly affect the meaning of
the text.[10]

Discovery doesn't always prove something right away. Discoveries
build upon each other. With the discovery of the Dead Sea Scrolls,
each fragment, each scroll, provides further insight. It joins pieces of
the biblical puzzle together. And these pieces tend to confirm what
we believe, the integrity of the Old Testament Scriptures. As the
pieces join, we're able to read the Bible with increasing confidence
in its veracity.

For those who, like us, believe the claims of the Bible and try to
incorporate its principles into daily living, discoveries like these bring
joy. For the skeptic or the person who's really never thought about
it, these discoveries provide much to think about, eventually leading
to the question all of us must answer: if this book not only contains
great principles from a great teacher but also contains very real claims
from an apparently real God, then what?

When our "So what?" becomes a "Now what?" we're confronted
with something very dynamic indeed.

# CHAPTER 10

# THE NEW SCRIPTURES

*"How foolish you are, how slow you are to believe everything the prophets said! Was it not necessary for the Messiah to suffer these things and then to enter his glory?" And Jesus explained to them what was said about himself in all the Scriptures, beginning with the books of Moses and the writings of all the prophets.*

—LUKE 24:25–27 GNT

*He told us about Christ's disciples being fishermen, and we were left to assume, as my brother and I did, that all first-class fishermen on the Sea of Galilee were fly fishermen and that John, the favorite, was a dry-fly fisherman.*

—NORMAN MACLEAN,
*A RIVER RUNS THROUGH IT*

*I am a Jew, but I am enthralled by the luminous figure of the Nazarene. . . . No one can read the Gospels without feeling the actual presence of Jesus. His personality pulsates in every word. No myth is filled with such life.*

—ALBERT EINSTEIN[1]

I magine someone routinely wrote you letters every month. The letters gave you great advice about living your life. You benefited not only in your personal life but also in your professional life.

Over time, you came to love the monthly letters. You kept them in a safe place in your home office. You returned to their contents often. You shared some of them with your friends and read them aloud to your family.

They especially helped you through some tough times, like when you lost your dad to cancer. That one letter about hope—so good, so deep, so perfect for the moment.

And what about that letter that talked about how that very hope you loved to read about so much was coming soon. And it was actually going to be in the form of a person, a kind of leader in your community. He was going to bring a beautiful hope to everyone. And the letter promised this; it didn't just give you platitudes never to be fulfilled.

You couldn't wait to hear more. To meet this person. When was he arriving?

But then, one day, the letters stopped arriving in your mailbox. Maybe there was a mix-up at the post office. Or maybe the sender wanted some time off. You told yourself, *Surely, the letter will arrive tomorrow.*

*Next month for sure*, you thought. *It will arrive. Why would the sender signal hope of this magnitude and then disappear?*

116

But one skipped month turned into another. And another. The next letter never came.

After a few months, you stopped looking for it. A few months later, you forgot all about the letters. You stopped returning to past letters for encouragement.

Now you go about your business as if those letters never came in the first place. Sometimes your friends ask you about the letters, but you try to change the subject. You do a little remembering with them but brush their message of hope away, as if they were nothing more than a fancy, a myth.

Years later, your children discover your box of neatly kept letters in your study.

"What's this?" asks your daughter.

"Nothing. Just some old letters I forgot to get rid of."

"There's so many of them. Who are they from? What are they about?"

"No one and nothing. Just throw them away."

But your daughter doesn't throw them away. She keeps the box and takes it to her house. She spends an entire weekend reading a year's worth of the letters. She laughs and cries and falls in love with the message of the letters.

One day, she returns for a visit.

"I need to confess something," she says. "I took your box of letters home. I didn't throw them out."

"Well . . . that's fine, I guess. Have you read any?"

"Oh yes. I've read many of them. They're so wonderful. So filled with hope."

"Yes, I used to think that too," you reply. "You can keep them if you want. They do carry a special something."

"Do you think this person the letters discuss will ever come? I mean, it seems almost too good to be true."

"I'm not sure. I used to wait with anticipation about his coming. But so much time has passed."

Your daughter leaves and returns home. Over time, she and her husband have their own family. They get old, and their kids find the letters. And the same conversation ensues.

What if this went on for four hundred years?

What would happen to the stories found in those letters? And what if the culture was different than our icon-driven culture of immediacy? What if storytelling was the culture? What if stories were passed down through generations and recorded by special people trained to copy the stories and letters that were passed on?

Now imagine the four hundred years have passed, and your distant relative readies for work and heads out to the shoreline to prep his boat for another day of fishing. He's on the beach, working on his fishing gear, when some stranger walks up to him.

"Come with me. I'll make a new kind of fisherman out of you. I'll show you how to catch men and women instead of perch and bass."

Something's weird about this guy. He talks unlike anyone your relative has ever met. He possesses a strange confidence. But your relative follows him and quickly learns that this strange man claims to be the very person from the letters. Four hundred years of silence, and then this man shows up claiming to be the long-awaited one. The one who will set captives free and bring hope to everyone.

Your relative thinks about all the generations before him. How they all longed for this exact moment. And now here he is, face-to-face with Hope itself.

## Fulfilled Promises

When you open the New Testament today, the first four books you will find are called the Gospels. Each gives a unique account and

perspective of the life of Jesus. And, interestingly, the New Testament
is geared with a multiplicity of readers in mind. Matthew geared his
account for a Jewish readership. The books of Mark and Luke were
written for gentile readers.

And then there is Luke's gospel. If the physician and friend of Paul
the apostle was indeed the author of Luke, it would make him the only
gentile author included in the New Testament. Luke, as it's commonly
held, also wrote the book of Acts. Most scholars recommend looking at
these two books as part 1 and part 2, referring to them as Luke-Acts.[2]
The book of Luke gives the account of Jesus' life and ministry, while
Acts tells about the church Jesus instituted through his followers, and
the miraculous way the news of Jesus' death and resurrection spread
literally throughout the world.

The gospel of John was written much later, sometime around
AD 90–100, while John—the Beloved Disciple—was living in the
city known as Ephesus. He wrote to a broad audience—to Christians
everywhere. John, arguably, also wrote three short letters known as
John 1, 2, and 3. And he wrote one of the most interesting books in
the New Testament, Revelation. John was part of Jesus' inner circle.
Tradition tells us he was boiled alive in oil and then exiled to the island
of Patmos, where he penned Revelation.

As we showed in an earlier chapter, the Old Testament connects with
the New Testament. We showed how the prophet Isaiah foretold the
way in which Jesus would die—seven hundred years before it happened.
Then, in the gospel accounts, we see Jesus living out those words.

The New Testament is a promise fulfilled.

Four hundred years stand between the final writings of the Old
Testament and the New Testament. The man called Jesus emerges
out of an obscure Galilean community, making claims that shocked
the leaders of Israel. The statements continue to shock and divide
the world. He was a walking fulfillment of what many anticipated.

Because of the politically charged climate of Jesus' time, many Jews looked for someone to emerge who would deliver their nation back to its former glory.

The Gospels present Jesus as this Messiah. But more than a political leader—a leader for all of humanity. This not only shocked the Jewish leaders of his day; it shocks many people now. Jesus, our deliverer? Our redeemer? Our savior?

Is it just religious talk, or is it really the fulfillment of thousands of years of promise and expectation?

## Overwhelming Evidence

In his bestselling book *The New Evidence That Demands a Verdict*, Josh McDowell delivers a convincing argument regarding the manuscript evidence of the New Testament as compared with the manuscript evidence for some of the world's classic works of literature. McDowell includes a statement made by Sir Frederic Kenyon, former rector and principal librarian of the British Museum, who says it's believed we possess accurate texts of all seven of Sophocles' works: *Ajax, Antigone, The Women of Trachis, Oedepus Rex, Electra, Philocretes,* and *Oedepus at Colonus.*

"But," he continues, "the earliest substantial manuscript upon which it is based was written more than 1400 years after the poet's death."[3] Contrast the works of the great classical writer Sophocles with the manuscripts we possess of the New Testament. We possess over 5,700 manuscripts of the New Testament. As if the number of manuscripts were not enough, Sir Frederic Kenyon says, "In no other case is the interval of time between the composition of the book and the date of the earliest extant manuscript so short as that of the New Testament."

When you consider that the New Testament was written during

the latter part of the first century and that the earliest manuscripts date from the third and fourth centuries, it at first seems a long time. But when you compare the three hundred to four hundred years with the Sophocles manuscript interval of fourteen hundred years, it's not even a fair comparison. Yet is anyone arguing for the inaccuracy of the Sophocles plays because of such a wide interval?

The earliest manuscripts for the New Testament are the Codex Sinaiticus, currently held at the British Library in London, and the Codex Vaticanus, currently held at the Vatican in Rome. Both, it's believed, come from the fourth century. The Codex Vaticanus contains a higher quality of text and contains most of the New Testament.

Though no original autographs of the biblical authors have survived, the manuscripts of the New Testament continue to gain evidence for their reliability. The letter that Paul the apostle wrote to the Galatian Christians is one of the earliest writings, along with an early church creed found in Paul's letter to Christians in Corinth (1 Cor. 15:1–8), which some estimate to have been written around AD 36, a mere few years after Jesus' recorded death and resurrection.

Evidence will continue to mount. But perhaps the most significant expression of the New Testament's veracity lies in how deeply the teachings of Jesus have impacted individuals and communities. Jesus can be a polarizing figure. Some still doubt his existence. Yet most scholars today recognize that the man Jesus of Nazareth did walk this earth.

Jesus' life and teachings continue to inspire many. In 1926, Dr. James Allan Francis gave a memorable sermon to the Baptist Young People's Union at a Los Angeles convention. A friend transcribed it and titled it "Arise, Sir Knight." Though Dr. Francis later published the sermon in a book titled *The Real Jesus and Other Sermons,* many in the Christian tradition know the edited version of this sermon as "One Solitary Life." The popular piece reads,

Here is a man who was born in an obscure village, the child of a peasant woman.

He grew up in another obscure village, where He worked in a carpenter shop until He was thirty, and then for three years He was an itinerant preacher.

He never wrote a book. He never held an office. He never owned a home. He never had a family. He never went to college.

He never put his foot inside a big city. He never traveled two hundred miles from the place where He was born. He never did one of the things that usually accompany greatness.

He had no credentials but Himself. He had nothing to do with this world except the naked power of His divine manhood.

While still a young man, the tide of public opinion turned against Him. His friends ran away. One of them denied Him.

He was turned over to His enemies. He went through the mockery of a trial. He was nailed to a cross between two thieves. His executioners gambled for the only piece of property He had on earth while He was dying—and that was his coat.

When he was dead He was taken down and laid in a borrowed grave through the pity of a friend. Nineteen wide centuries have come and gone and today He is the centerpiece of the human race and the leader of the column of progress.

I am far within the mark when I say that all the armies that ever marched, and all the navies that ever were built, and all the parliaments that ever sat, all the kings that ever reigned, put together have not affected the life of man upon this earth as powerfully as has that One Solitary Life.[4]

As Dr. Francis points out, Jesus did not do what others have done to become known. Therefore you will not see his image on a coin, or his name listed as a military or political leader. So what evidence do we have for Jesus?

If we look outside the New Testament writings, we find other writings—like those of Lucian of Somosata, Suetonius, and others—that speak of Jesus and his followers. One of the more well-known writings is of the Jewish historian Josephus. Josephus provides us with important information about the cultural world in which Jesus lived. We gain understanding about "the social, political, and historical scene and religious backgrounds of the New Testament."[5]

Another is of Cornelius Tacitus. Tacitus is considered the greatest historian of ancient Rome. He lived from AD 55–120. Here's what Tacitus says about Jesus:

> But not all the relief that could come from man, not all the bounties that the prince could bestow, nor all the atonements which could be presented to the gods, availed to relieve Nero from the infamy of being believed to have ordered the conflagration, the fire of Rome. Hence, to suppress the rumor, he falsely charged with the guilt, and punished with the most exquisite tortures, the persons commonly called Christians, who were hated for their enormities. Christus, the founder of the name, was put to death by Pontius Pilate, procurator of Judea in the reign of Tiberius: but the pernicious superstition, repressed for a time, broke out again, not only through Judea, where the mischief originated, but through the city of Rome also (*Annals* XV, 44).[6]

Furthermore, Edwin Yamauchi writes in his book *Jesus Under Fire* that we could set the New Testament aside and we'd still discover illuminating facts about the man Jesus of Nazareth, such as:

(1) Jesus was a Jewish teacher;

(2) many people believed that he performed healings and exorcisms;

(3) he was rejected by the Jewish leaders;

(4) he was crucified under Pontius Pilate in the reign of Tiberius;

(5) despite this shameful death, his followers, who believed that he was still alive, spread beyond Palestine so that there were multitudes of them in Rome by AD 64;

(6) all kinds of people from the cities and countryside—men and women, slave and free—worshiped him as God by the beginning of the second century.[7]

What do we do with this? Is this historical figure all that the New Testament claims he is?

# CHAPTER 11

# A SPECIAL BOOK

*I expect to pass through life but once. If therefore there be any kindness I can show, or any good thing that I can do to any fellow being, let me do it now, and not defer or neglect it, as I shall not pass this way again.*

—WILLIAM PENN[1]

*"Let the little children come to me, and do not hinder them, for the kingdom of God belongs to such as these."*

—MARK 10:14

*Many books in my library are now behind and beneath me. They were good in their way once, and so were the clothes I wore when I was ten years old; but I have outgrown them. Nobody ever outgrows Scripture; the book widens and deepens with our years.*

—CHARLES HADDON SPURGEON[2]

It was November of 2004. Steve and I took our five kids out to enjoy a hibachi dinner. We were celebrating my birthday. Derek, our oldest, was a senior in high school, Lauren was a junior, Lindy was in the eighth grade, Danielle was in the sixth grade, and Grace was four years old at the time.

We sat around the chef and watched him prepare the meal with flair.

There were eight seats around the table and seven of us.

Suddenly one of the girls said, "Mom, we think we need to adopt a baby from China!"

I said, "Wow! I love adoption. We have friends and family who have adopted, and we have supported that. It's a beautiful thing, but we have five kids already, and our quiver is full. You know how busy I am taking care of you five, homeschooling some of you and taking the rest of you back and forth to school, sports, and church activities. I'm so busy, and Dad works hard and has to travel a lot. Our lives are so full already."

They weren't impressed or inhibited.

"Yeah, but we think we need to adopt a baby."

Notice the "we" they used. We, not me and Steve.

"Well, that's really awesome. Maybe God is calling you to adopt when you grow up. If he is, you need to make sure that whoever your spouse is feels called to adopt too."

I was just trying to have a conversation with them and listen to their desires. But in my heart, I was not feeling like this was for us at that time. I tried to dissuade them and blow it off, but Lauren and Lindy were particularly insistent.

"Just think, you could be saving a life. You could change a life forever."

"I love that idea," I replied. "Absolutely! I just don't feel like I am called to adopt. Look around this table. I have five children—seven of us around this table. We fill it up. Do you see any tables around us with one family filling up the entire table? The other tables have several families around them. We take up one all by ourselves."

"But there is one empty chair."

They had me there, but I still kept the notion at arm's length.

"You know, guys, that I love adoption. I love children. I love family."

And we do. We know many families who have adopted; we have supported others who have adopted their children through the years. This wasn't a new concept for us.

I said, "You know, if God's calling us to adopt, he is going to call me. I know that you can't imagine it now, but you will grow up and have your own lives and families. If I adopt a child, I'll be their mother for the rest of my life. I will fill that role the rest of my days. It's different for me than it will be for you guys."

"Well, we will help! We have so much love to give. We have room in our home and in our hearts! Will you just think about it, Mom?" They even picked out a name.

"Okay," I said. "I'll think about it." In my mind, I was wondering where this new passion for adoption was coming from.

Derek, our oldest, just sat there rather quiet.

"Come on, Derek. Would you really want five sisters?"

He didn't even hesitate. "Yeah, why not? I'd like another sister."

I was a little surprised at my family's certainty and enthusiasm. We were already a big group!

I said, "Okay. Look, guys, I'll think about it. Just don't get your hopes up. Maybe God is calling you to adopt someday. Now let's get back to celebrating my birthday!"

So we left it at that. Or at least I did.

## Talking to God about Adoption

A few weeks later, at our big Thanksgiving family celebration, the issue went to the next level. The kids evidently said something around their grandma about adopting. Afterward my mother called and said, "The girls mentioned you are adopting."

"Oh no." I chuckled. "There has been some discussion. I told the kids that I'd think about it, but I don't really see it happening."

I called the kids in and told them, "You can't tell people that we are going to adopt, because I don't know if it will ever happen."

"Will you at least pray about it, Mom?" they asked.

"Okay, I'll make you a deal: I'll be open and pray about it, but you can't put pressure on me or talk to people about it."

"Okay, Mom!" they replied as they smiled at each other, like it was already a done deal.

We got through the busy holidays and many evenings spent at basketball games for two of my teenagers. In January, Lindy came to me while I was fixing dinner in the kitchen.

"Hey, Mom. I just wanted to ask if you have been praying about adopting."

"You know, to be honest with you, I haven't seriously spent much time talking to God about it. But I told you I would, so now that the holidays are over, I will. I will take it more seriously and do what I told you I would do."

"Okay, great! Thanks, Mom!" she said.

## From Praying to Weeping

I started reading and researching online about adoption. I read reviews of different agencies and many blogs of families who had adopted. I ordered books to read about adoption. This time, I seriously prayed and actively thought about it.

By the end of February, I realized this was something that was really heavy on my heart. At first it was more of a commitment to follow through with what I told my children I would do. My attitude was, *Okay, I'll pray about it; I'll look into it.*

Much to my surprise, adoption became the desire of my heart. When I opened my heart to really listen to what God wanted for our family, when I opened my mind to the reality of adopting a child, the emotions flooded in. It was never far from my thoughts. I could be in the shower, and it would pop into my thoughts, and I would weep. I would be driving down the road, and it would come over me like a flood, and I would start crying. My heart was overflowing with new emotions. I realized, *This just keeps coming to my mind out of the blue. Something is going on. Maybe God is trying to get my attention.*

It kept hitting me at random times and places.

I said, "God, are you trying to tell me something?"

I read another book and more blogs. I finally called a couple of agencies about adoption requirements. The first one I called was in Oklahoma.

"How many kids do you have?" they asked.

I answered, "Five."

"Well, you can't adopt from China, because they have a rule that won't let you have five kids in your home and adopt another one."

"I didn't realize that."

"The only thing we can do is send a letter to their government agency that handles adoption policies and ask for permission. Let's wait and see what they say."

"All right," I replied. "It doesn't hurt to ask. I'll wait to hear back from you."

They sent the letter.

I called another agency out of state that had caught my interest. I said, "I would like to get some information about adopting. I'm not sure if we would qualify, but we are considering adopting a baby. We are thinking about an adoption from China."

"Sure," they replied. "So, you have five kids at home?"

"Yes, I do," I said.

"How old is your oldest child? Will they be moving out anytime soon?"

"As a matter of fact, our oldest is eighteen. He is a senior and will be moving to college this fall," I responded.

"It shouldn't be any problem, then," they said.

Surprised, I replied, "Are you sure? I called another agency, and they didn't give me much hope for us to be approved."

"I'm quite sure. Let me mail you a packet of information."

"Well, I don't know if we are to that point yet."

"How about we mail you a packet, and you can read through it. If you have any further questions, you can call us back."

So I checked the mail each day until the packet arrived. I didn't want the kids to know we were receiving this packet. I was afraid of getting their hopes up and it not working out. And, quite frankly, I was still trying to wrap my mind around the idea of adopting and having six kids.

However, the idea was beginning to take hold. There were many nights when I would stay up late, after the kids were in bed, and read online about other people's adoption experiences. The anticipation was building.

In late February, Steve and I went out for a dinner date. We tried to get out about once a month for date nights alone. I remember thinking, *I really feel like we're supposed to do this, but I have no idea what Steve's thoughts are. He never said anything when the kids were talking about it all through my birthday dinner.*

It had been four months since my epic birthday dinner conversation, and Steve had never said anything about his thoughts regarding us adopting at this point. I wondered what that meant, but with a house full of busy kids, we didn't get a lot of time to have deep discussions.

"I have something I have been wanting to ask you," I said as we ate our meal. "You remember when the kids brought up us adopting last November? I have been reading and researching about adopting, and I need to know how you feel about it. I realized that you've never mentioned anything about it."

I remember his response vividly still today. He put his fork down and looked at me and said, "I could get really excited about it."

Chill bumps. I knew at that moment that we were going to adopt our sixth child.

## Taking Steps

"What do you think about going to this workshop to learn more about it?" I asked.

"I think we should do it," Steve replied.

So we did.

We didn't tell anyone where we were going as I arranged childcare. We didn't even tell our kids what we were doing that day. Our two oldest knew that we would be at their formal junior-senior banquet that evening. I had been on the committee planning it for months, with many late nights of working to make it perfect. It was a big deal for us!

When we left for the workshop that morning, we just said, "See you at the banquet!" We had to go from the all-day workshop straight to the banquet venue, forty-five minutes away, with our change of clothes in the car. We didn't get home until after midnight, knowing that we had church early the next morning.

That was Saturday night, April 9. Steve had filled out the application that day and signed at the bottom. I was a little nervous about it. I said, "What are you doing? We haven't made a definite decision yet!" Looking back, it was only me who had not made a decision.

Before we turned in for the night, I said, "Steve, I've got this legal pad with about twenty questions regarding adoption. Can I just ask you a few before we go to bed, sort of like an interview? This is really weighing on my heart."

"Okay," he said.

I knew that inside he was really thinking, *We have church in the morning, it's getting late, and you want to talk?* He's a good man. I ended my "interview" when his eyes began to cross.

"Do you feel like God is calling you to adopt? Do you feel like you would ever feel any differently toward an adopted child versus a biological child?"

"I know I won't have any problem with it; my sister was adopted."

"Oh yeah, she is." He was not new to being an adoptive family. The list went on.

I peppered him with questions that I thought were essential for us to think through. We talked until 2:00 a.m. That night, I remember praying, "God, it would be so great if you would give me a dream so I would have my answer and know what we are supposed to do."

I dreamed about everything we had heard in the workshop, but I didn't have a specific, clear "dream from God." I have had experiences with those before, so I was disappointed when I woke up to get ready for church. I started getting all of the kids ready, but I was exhausted.

"Steve, I'm worn out from so many late nights planning the kids' banquet. Would you mind if I stayed home this morning to catch up on rest? I'm totally spent from this last week."

"That's no problem. Why don't you just meet us for lunch?"

I thought, *I'll get everyone out the door, rest a little more, and meet them later.* It felt strange to send my family on without me to church, but my body was telling me it desperately needed more rest. Also, we were leaving at 5:00 a.m. the next morning as chaperones for the high school senior trip to New York City, and there was much to be done.

In the quiet house, I stood by my bed and openly talked to God.

"God, I feel like I'm running from your will, and I really don't want to do that. I've analyzed this idea to death, and I feel like you are trying to tell me something. I'm not going to question this anymore. I don't need to have it all figured out. I'm going to move forward and run with it. I only ask you for one thing: clarity."

I felt peace.

## Does God Speak through Dreams?

I slept a little bit and woke up feeling refreshed. I went to meet my family for lunch.

During lunch, Steve randomly asked me if I had the phone number for a gentleman we know at our church.

I said, "No, I don't have his number."

"Well, you need to call him," Steve said.

"Why do I need to call him?" I asked. It seemed like a strange request.

"You just need to call him," Steve persisted.

"Why don't *you* call him? What's this about?"

"I'm not telling you. You just need to talk to him," he said.

"Okay." I was chuckling because I didn't understand what this was all about. It was unusual for Steve to ask me to call a guy from church for no apparent reason. I tried my very best to get him to explain, but he wasn't budging. I couldn't get Lindy or Danielle to tell me either. They had evidently been with Steve at the church when he ran into this gentleman.

"Lauren, can you get his number from Michael?" I asked. (Michael later became Lauren's husband.)

Lauren got the number and gave it to me. As we were leaving, I said, "Steve, what's this about? I'm not leaving until you tell me."

"Well, I'll see you at home, then." He laughed.

There I stood in the parking lot by my car, laughing and trying to figure out what was going on with my husband.

*This is crazy*, I thought.

I got in my car and made the call.

"Hey, Jackie, Steve wanted me to tell you what we talked about at church today. I know this is going to sound crazy."

"Great! He wouldn't tell me what you discussed. What's this about?"

"Now, listen," he said. "I was raised in a Baptist church, and I don't know much about the whole 'word from the Lord' kind of thing. I'm new to this, but I felt I was supposed to tell you guys something, and I didn't know how you would receive it. But when I ran into Steve after church, I knew I had to say something."

He continued, "You guys sit in the balcony and I sit on the floor level, and we don't typically see each other on Sunday morning. But today as I got out of my seat, I turned around, and there was Steve walking down the aisle right toward me. I knew God wanted me to tell you guys this.

"Last week in my Bible study, I felt like God was saying, 'There's a blessing for Steve and Jackie in China,' so whatever you're doing, keep doing it."

I could hardly believe what I was hearing.

God gave me the clarity I had asked for just a few hours before. I knew at that moment we were moving forward with adoption.

He continued, "I don't understand it, but I just knew that I was supposed to tell you guys."

"You know what?" I replied. "I understand it. Did Steve tell you what we did yesterday?"

"Yes, he told me you guys went to a workshop and that he filled out an application."

"That's right. He signed the papers to begin the adoption process, but I didn't. This morning, I prayed and asked God for clarity. I know why you were supposed to tell us this."

It was time to call a family meeting. When I got home, I called everyone together in the kitchen.

"Family meeting time! We have something to discuss!" I filled the kids in on the day's revelation. Then I started with Derek. "You're the oldest, so why don't you go first. What do you think we should do?"

"Well, Mom, I think you know what you're supposed to do," he said.

"Okay, anybody else have anything to add?"

The girls all looked at me wide-eyed. Nobody else had anything to add. Looking back, I wonder if their young minds were fully processing how God had answered their nightly prayers on that day.

"All right! Meeting dismissed."

It was just like God said to me, "You asked for clarity, and here it is. Now run with it."

The day that we filled out the paperwork to begin our adoption process was April 9, 2005. God answered my request for clarity so clearly the next morning.

## God's Plan Is Beautiful

Two days later, I began a journal with this line: "This journal is dedicated to a very special little girl who is destined to be our daughter. Born an ocean away, but in our hearts every day."

I kept thinking about how there had been other times in my life when I asked for clear direction from God and didn't receive it. He made it so clear this time, within a matter of hours, that I felt compelled to get the paperwork done and appointments made as quickly as possible. I felt a sense of urgency.

We got busy. Every time I would get one paper done, I was ready to send it off and get started on the next one. We submitted the paperwork to the agencies, scheduled home studies, gathered all of the required documents, and submitted everything to our agency in August 2005.

We were logged in September 2005. The first time we saw that precious little face was January 3, 2007.

Once we received the long-awaited photo with her referral, we were amazed when we read on the paper that her birthday was April 9, 2006. You know, it could have been 364 other days of the year, but it was April 9. When I looked back in my journal to confirm that we had filled out the paperwork on April 9, with God's confirmation within hours of my prayer, I felt like this was one more sign that he was directing our path.

We made the long trip to pick up our daughter in February 2007. Gabriella—her name means "woman of God" and "God is my strength" and is the name our kids picked out at the hibachi dinner—was placed in our arms on February 25, 2007. She was ten-and-a-half months old. When the orphanage director brought her to the door and called our names, she smiled and reached out to us like she had been waiting for us to get there.

The day we picked up Gabi.

That day was one of the best days ever! I felt so blessed to be Mommy to this amazing baby girl. She cut her first tooth on the top within those first few days of bonding and began pulling up in her crib. I remember rocking her and thanking God that I hadn't missed out on this opportunity. I recall feeling like our adoption journey was one of the biggest faith walks I had ever taken at that time in my life.

We didn't know what the outcome would be, but God did, and he was with us all the way.

When we think back to that providential hibachi dinner, we can see how God was working his plans for us a year and a half before our daughter was even born.

Our decision to be an adoptive family was so enriching in all of our lives. I feel like I have an even better understanding of what it means in Ephesians 1:5, where it says, "God destined us to be his adopted children through Jesus Christ because of his love" (CEB).

Just as I loved my daughter from the moment she was placed in my arms, God loved me. Not because of anything I had accomplished, not because I did anything to earn his love, but because he chose to love me. It's a beautiful thing.

For our family, the Bible provides not only guidance for everyday life but also insight into God's heart for the helpless, those on the margins of life. We experienced how the Bible, as God's living word to us, inspired, guided, and confirmed specific direction with regard to our adoption of our daughter.

This wonderful book stands on its own in an academic setting and endears itself in a personal setting. It's a book that continually wows leaders, inspires the hopeless, and guides those of us lost in doubt and confusion. I am so grateful to have this wonderful guidebook for all of life's journeys that I have been on, and for those to come.

As people read our adoption story, we imagine there might be varying responses. One of those responses will be a sense of affinity. There are those who know exactly what we experienced, because they have experienced the same thing. Oh, the facts of the stories are different, but there is the same heartfelt belief that God was in the middle of the situation.

This isn't anything new. Throughout time, those who believe in the God of the Bible have claimed that he directed events in their lives. This kind of claim is called providence, defined as the foreseeing care and guidance of God. This idea was acknowledged often in the early days of our nation.

# PART 4

# APPEAL TO HEAVEN

שְׂאוּ־מָרוֹם
עֵינֵיכֶם

*Lift up your eyes and look to the heavens: Who created all these?*
*He who brings out the starry host one by one and calls forth each*
*of them by name.*

—ISAIAH 40:26

*The Bible teaches that God is love. Love includes communication.*
*Both Old and New Testaments teach that God speaks to us because*
*he loves us.*

—VISHAL MANGALWADI, *THE BOOK*
*THAT MADE YOUR WORLD*

CHAPTER 12

# REVOLUTION: THE BIBLE AND AMERICA

*That at the name of Jesus every knee should bow, in heaven and on earth and under the earth.*

—PHILIPPIANS 2:10

*To understand the American founding, one should study the works and deeds of the founders, both individually and collectively, and for additional insights into the founders' political insight into the culture, read the Bible.*

—DANIEL L. DREISBACH, *READING THE BIBLE WITH THE FOUNDING FATHERS*

*We are a community, a beloved community, all of us. Our individual fates are linked, our futures intertwined. And if we act in that knowledge and in that spirit, together, as the Bible says, we can move mountains.*

—JIMMY CARTER'S STATE OF THE UNION ADDRESS, JANUARY 19, 1978[1]

You live in colonial America. It's 1763, and things couldn't be better. Your colony in Massachusetts Bay? Thriving. Work's good in the timber industry, and your oldest just headed off to Harvard College to study the law. For nearly a decade, however, your family dealt with the unrest of war. But all that's settled down now.

Though people are a bit weary, being fresh off Britain's defeat of France in the Seven Years' War, around the colony there's a general feel of hope. You celebrate the victory with your English friends and even discuss a new era of peace for England and her colonies in the Americas.

An American revolution? Not even a thought.

Who would ever have thought that something as insignificant as a tax placed on paper would flare up into a full rebellion?

The British too are tired from their war with the French. And your neighbor just told you it's taken a toll on the Crown's pocketbook. They're broke.

To refill their coffers, they intend to levy a new tax. The tax stipulates that "goods from newspapers to playing cards had to be printed on paper bearing a royal stamp, reflecting the tax paid." Then the Crown also demands first rights to the Eastern White Pines—the choice wood you harvest for building masts for the king's navy. It's one thing to work hard harvesting the trees and receive fair wages along with a fair price for the wood. It's quite another to be bullied by the sovereign you build sailing vessels for.

You and other colonists articulate your ire through circulating the Latin motto *Nil desperandum Christo duce*, which translates "No need to fear with Christ as our leader." You remind the king that the sovereignty of God was the highest court in the land. Your pine tree symbol printed on the flag—the symbol of colonial resistance—says, "Appeal to Heaven."[2]

Tensions grow. As does the grip of tyranny.

Your family moved to the New World years ago for a chance to live free, to work hard, and to worship how they felt led. Now the dream of a place that's untangled from the heavy hand of the Crown is threatened.

What if we told you the Bible and pluralism worked hand in hand in the colonists' pursuit of freedom? What if we told you that diversity in thought was the result of a biblical underpinning enjoyed by the colonialists? What if we told you America grew strong roots because of its ability to hold differing views in a healthy tension, with the common goal of political and religious freedom? Would you believe it?

## A Healthy Society

Baylor historian Thomas Kidd reminds us that before, during, and after the Revolutionary War, Americans represented a patchwork quilt of religious beliefs and yet remained joined in foundational common causes.

Though Thomas Jefferson had unorthodox views of the Bible, he still embraced many biblical ideas. Many men and women who did not share an evangelical view of certain events, like George Washington's crossing of the Delaware, as an act of God's immediate providence and favor still embraced the basic tenets of the Bible.

In their differences, men like Jefferson, whom some called an infidel or atheist, and the Baptist minister John Leland found common ground on biblical principles of equality, religious freedom, a separate role for the church and the state, and the intrinsic worth of all people regardless of ethnicity or religion.

In fact, Thomas Jefferson viewed religious freedom as one of the primary needs of our new nation, and the protection of that liberty as crucial. Consider this letter "to the Society of the Methodist Episcopal Church at New London, Connecticut (February 4, 1809)." Among other things in the letter, Jefferson highlights the importance of protecting religious liberties. He writes,

> No provision in our constitution ought to be dearer to man than that which protects the rights of conscience against the enterprises of the civil authority. It has not left the religion of its citizens under the power of its public functionaries, were it possible that any of these should consider a conquest over the consciences of men either attainable or applicable to any desirable purpose. To me, no information could be more welcome than that the minutes of the several religious societies should prove, of late, larger additions than have been usual, to their several associations, and I trust that the whole course of my life has proved me a sincere friend to religious as well as civil liberty.

This letter was written one month before Jefferson left office. Apparently, he had received a letter of commendation for his service as president from the church he is addressing. As he points out in the first line of the second paragraph, he believed that no provision of the Constitution should be dearer than our religious freedom. That was the provision he was most proud of.

To the Society of the Methodist Episcopal church at New London. Connecticut

The approbation you are so good as to express of the measures which have been recommended & pursued during the course of my admi-nistration of the national concerns, is highly acceptable, the approving voice of our fellow citizens, for endeavors to be useful, is the greatest of all earthly rewards.

No provision in our constitution ought to be dearer to man, than that which protects the rights of conscience, against the enter-prizes of the civil authority. it has not left the religion of it's citizens under the power of it's public functionaries, were it possible that any of these should consider a conquest over the consciences of men either attainable, or applicable to any desirable purpose. to me, no information could be more welcome than that the minutes of the several religious societies should prove, of late, larger ad-ditions, than have been usual, to their several associations: and I trust that the whole course of my life has proved me a sincere friend to religious, as well as civil liberty.

I thank you for your affectionate good wishes for my future happiness. retirement is become essential to it: and one of it's best consolations will be to witness the advancement of my country in all those pursuits & acquisitions which constitute the character of a wise & virtuous nation: and I offer sincere prayers to heaven that it's benedictions may attend yourselves, our country, & all it's sons.

Th. Jefferson
Feb. 4. 1809.

Thomas Jefferson's letter to the Society of the Methodist
Episcopal Church at New London, Connecticut,
February 4, 1809 (National Christian Foundation).

Our family understands the value of religious freedom all too well. Let us give an example of religious freedoms and our own family. In September of 2012, our entire family gathered for a meeting about our family business, Hobby Lobby. On January 1, 2013, our health plan would be required to comply with the Affordable Care Act mandate that would force us to provide and pay for four potentially life-terminating drugs and devices. We gathered with heavy hearts, knowing that this was something we could not accept.

The line we drew in the sand would cost us over one million dollars per day in fines. And if we held our ground, it had the potential to end our company. Nearly all family members voiced their opinions. It was unanimous. We had to stick to our beliefs no matter what the cost.

And so began our almost two-year journey with our country's court system that ended with the U.S. Supreme Court deciding in our favor. Thomas Jefferson's words never felt more real than on that day when we heard the court's decision.

In its infancy, America was a place where people of all walks of life and all religious affiliations could get along with one another. The key was the agreement to build the society according to principles found in the Bible.

Of course, we can't and won't hide our own faith tradition. That's the beauty of our country. Each person possesses the freedom to pursue their own religion. But we also can't get away from our history as a country founded upon principles primarily from the Judeo-Christian tradition.

That's not a statement meant to ruffle feathers. It's a simple fact. We're not saying, "We are a Christian nation." You would first have to define what you mean by a Christian nation. But we are saying this incredible book we call the Bible affected many great men and women who came to this country seeking religious freedom and a fresh start on life.

For the most part, they built this nation from a biblical worldview. Imagine if our country's founders had a Hindu, Muslim, or atheistic worldview. Our nation would look much different.

## Five Ideas That Built a Nation

Many of the founders were influenced by the Bible's teachings. To some, that might sound like a radical statement. But Kidd gives us five biblical ideas that "connected far-flung and widely varied Americans"[3] (sounds like America today!).

The first biblical idea is *no state churches*. Evangelicals sounded this bell more than others, but they found a close ally in the likes of Jefferson. It is evident in the constitutional provision he praises in his letter. The taste of state-sponsored churches lingered in the mouths of many British colonists. This biblical idea infused our country with an abundance of denominations, all free to pursue their own religious convictions.

The second biblical idea is *the idea of a creator God as the guarantor of fundamental human rights*. It was Jefferson's pen that introduced the world to this radical idea that all men are created equal, endowed by their Creator with certain unalienable rights. This particular idea carried weight among the colonists, who recognized the hand of a tyrant when they saw one.

Rights by creation also played a major role in the abolition of slavery. If God created man in his own image, as it says in the book of Genesis (1:27), then how could anyone justify enslaving another person? God created everyone, and so everyone possessed rights as a God-created individual. Unfortunately, in early America not all fully embraced this idea. While slavery had been a part of human history, the idea of equality was growing. Though it took far too long for the nation to embrace this truth, its foundation was there from the beginning.

The third biblical idea might sound odd to many because we don't use the word *sin* much anymore in the mainstream. The idea is that *human sinfulness posed a threat to our civil government.* Early Americans rejected centralized power in government. This was the way of the British Crown, not the new American government. Today, our states possess a certain level of autonomy, and at the federal level, power is divided between the three branches of government. This was thought to be vital for the survival of our government. Americans believed all men were created equal, but "all men were not angels."[4]

The colonists' awareness of human nature played a vital role in shaping America's governmental architecture. Without this awareness, government and its officials would grow corrupt. But awareness of man's corruption—again, another biblical idea (Rom. 3:23)—was worthless without taking the next step, which leads to Kidd's fourth biblical idea.

The fourth biblical idea ties into the third: *a republic needed to be sustained by virtue.* Kidd reminds us how well centralized government controls people, keeping them in line. But Americans witnessed this kind of governance and knew it led to tyranny. So how would a country work if power was dispersed? Who would control the masses when they ran wild?

Enter virtue—behavior showing high moral standards.

Early American leaders, like Samuel Adams, believed that if we as a nation remained virtuous, we could achieve greatness. He even called this pinnacle of greatness a "Christian Sparta." Virtuous living requires accountability, checks and balances. Once virtue erodes, however, the system risks failure.

Dr. William Bennett, author of *The Moral Compass,* reminds us, "The success of any organization depends on the character of its citizens."[5] The success of America, or any democratic republic, depends on each person taking responsibility for their actions, exercising loyalty to family, friends, and government, taking up the rigors of honest work, and employing the virtue of self-discipline. In our finest moments as a nation, these virtuous characteristics did not merely emerge from nowhere. They shone from a people who understood the value of good character.

On the contrary, a culture of complainers usually signifies self-ishness. Bennett says when a person focuses primarily on their own needs, they fail at being a good citizen. When we encounter good citizens, we usually experience the virtues associated with selflessness. When we remember the heroic acts of the first responders on 9/11, we often choke back tears. It is interesting how the selfless act inspires and touches us so deeply, while the selfish act repulses us. Our second president, John Adams, well noted, "Our Constitution was made only for a moral and religious people. It is wholly inadequate to the government of any other."

The fifth biblical idea is *the belief that God moved in and through nations.*

In his book *The American Miracle: Divine Providence in the Rise of the Republic,* Michael Medved documents, time and time again, events during America's formation that are credited to providence.

America is not perfect; it never has been and it never will be. But America has been the most successful nation in history. More lives in this nation, and around the world, have been improved as a result of its success.

On July 9, 1755, during the French and Indian War, the British Army, led by General Braddock, was marching to the French-controlled Fort Duquesne, which later became the city of Pittsburgh.

The French and Indians, knowing they were outnumbered, determined that an ambush would help their odds of winning a battle.

Several miles from the fort, in a wooded area, the ambush took place. Over two-thirds of the French and Indian militia were Indians, skilled in the art of ambush and guerilla warfare.

The battle was a rout.

Both sides were stunned as a result. General Braddock, furious about the tactics used by the French and Indians, insisted his army form regular platoons and columns, as military rules prescribed. To do anything less would be to show a lack of courage and discipline. General Braddock had five horses shot out from under him in the battle before he himself was shot and wounded. A few days later, he died.

During the battle, the Indians made special efforts to shoot at the officers who were on horseback, knowing that targeting the leadership would benefit their cause. All but one of the mounted officers were shot. That officer was one of General Braddock's aides, George Washington.

After the battle, George Washington, at age twenty-three, wrote to his mother and his brother. The following are his letters:

Honored Madam:

As I doubt not but you have heard of our defeat, and perhaps have it represented in a worse light (if possible) than it deserves, I have taken this earliest opportunity to give you some account of the engagement as it happened, within seven miles of the French fort, on Wednesday, the 9th inst.

We marched on to that place without any considerable loss, having only now and then a straggler picked up by the Indian scouts of the French. When we came there, we were attacked by a body of French and Indians, whose number (I am certain) did not exceed 300 men. Ours consisted of about 1,300 well-armed troops, chiefly of the English soldiers, who were struck with such a panic that they behaved with more cowardice than it is possible to conceive. The officers behaved gallantly in order to encourage their men, for which they suffered greatly, there being near 60 killed and wounded—a large proportion out of the number we had!

The Virginia troops showed a good deal of bravery, and

were near all killed; for I believe out of three companies that were there, there are scarce 30 men left alive. Captain Peyrouny and all his officers, down to a corporal, were killed; Captain Polson shared near as hard a fate, for only one of his was left. In short, the dastardly behavior of those they call regulars exposed all others that were inclined to do their duty to almost certain death; and, at last, in despite of all the efforts of the officers to the contrary, they broke and ran as sheep pursued by dogs; and it was impossible to rally them.

The general was wounded; of which he died three days after. Sir Peter Halket was killed in the field, where died many other brave officers. I luckily escaped without a wound, though I had four bullets through my coat, and two horses shot under me. Captains Orme and Morris, two of the general's aides de camp, were wounded early in the engagement, which rendered the duty hard upon me, as I was the only person then left to distribute the general's orders; which I was scarcely able to do as I was not half recovered from a violent illness that confined me to my bed and a wagon for above ten days.

I am still in a weak and feeble condition; which induces me to halt here two or three days in hopes of recovering a little strength to enable me to proceed homeward; from whence I fear I shall not be able to stir till toward September, so that I shall not have the pleasure of seeing you till then, unless it be in Fairfax. . . .

P.S. We had about 300 men killed and as many, and more, wounded.[6]

Dear Brother,

As I have heard, since my arrival at this place, a circumstantial account of my death and dying speech, I take this early opportunity of contradicting the first, and of assuring you, that I have not, as yet, composed the latter. But, by the All-powerful Dispensations of Providence, I have been protected beyond all human probability or expectation; for I had four Bullets through my Coat, and two Horses shot under me; yet escaped unhurt, altho[ugh] Death was leveling my Companions on every side of me!

Fifteen years later, while Washington was exploring western territories, his party was approached by a company of Indians. The chief explained his desire to meet Washington through an interpreter. The following is the record of that conversation:

> I am chief and ruler over my tribes. My influence extends to the waters of the great lakes and to the far blue mountains. I have traveled a long and weary path that I might see the young warrior of the great battle. It was on the day when the white man's blood mixed with the streams of our forest that I first beheld this chief [Washington]. . . . I called to my young men and said . . . Quick, let your aim be certain, and he dies. Our rifles were leveled, rifles which, but for you, knew not how to miss—'twas all in vain, a power mightier far than we, shielded you. . . . I am come to pay homage to the man who is the particular favorite of Heaven, and who can never die in battle.

I believe, as so many of our country's founders did, that God's hand of providence was involved. Not only did they believe it, but they in fact risked their lives for it. So central was the concept of providence to our nation's founders that we find it front and center in our own Declaration of Independence: "And for the support of this Declaration, with a firm reliance on the protection of divine Providence, we mutually pledge to each other our Lives, our Fortunes and our sacred Honor."

# CHAPTER 13

# REVOLUTIONARY: A NATION OF THE BOOK

*These commandments that I give you today are to be on your hearts. Impress them on your children. Talk about them when you sit at home and when you walk along the road, when you lie down and when you get up.*

—DEUTERONOMY 6:6–7

*The Bible was one book that literate Americans in the seventeenth, eighteenth, and nineteenth centuries could be expected to know well. Biblical imagery provided the basic framework for imaginative thought in America up until quite recent times and, unconsciously, its control is still formidable.*

—ROBERT A. BELLAH

*I have read a fiery gospel writ in burnished rows of steel: / "As ye deal with my contemners, so with you my grace shall deal"; / Let the Hero, born of woman, crush the serpent with his heel, / Since God is marching on.*

—JULIA WARD HOWE,
"BATTLE HYMN OF THE REPUBLIC"

W e used to be a nation of the book. But not anymore.

So many people, it seems, view the Bible negatively in the public square. For us, hearing politicians quoting the Bible or alluding to the idea of a Judeo-Christian ethic makes perfect sense, for a number of reasons. But one reason is simply because we grew up with the book.

We often recognize the Bible when it's quoted or when someone alludes to its principles. We understand too that not all embrace our point of view. Our beautiful country brims full of folks from different faiths.

But what if we could, for just one moment, stand back and look at the Bible together?

Take in its history.

Consider its impact in our nation's founding.

Get to know its story better.

We, as a culture, are simply not well versed in the Bible, like our Revolutionary predecessors. Perhaps our differences appear sharp today because we lack the common ground enjoyed by the colonists. They grew up reading and knowing Scripture.

In his illuminating book *Reading the Bible with the Founding Fathers*, Daniel Dreisbach reminds us of just this point: "The American founders read the Bible."[1] The early Americans knew their Bibles. It was part of the curriculum for children in elementary schools. One British man wrote home to England and said, "There are very few really ignorant men in America. . . . They have all been *readers* from their youth up."

When Johannes Gutenberg printed the very first Bible, between 1452 and 1455, he didn't just initiate the advent of the bestselling book in world history. He also democratized its contents. Before Gutenberg, only the clergy read and taught the Bible's doctrines. With the Scriptures now in the "vulgar" (or common) languages, people could read it for themselves. If you wanted to be a contributor to society, it was a given that you knew the Bible.

## Biblical Wisdom Was Everywhere

By the time America was founded, biblical wisdom had become ubiquitous, not only to the general public but especially in political leadership. Proverbs 14:34 became a favorite wisdom saying for the likes of Samuel Adams and John Adams. The proverb reads, "Righteousness exalteth a nation" (KJV).

John Adams invoked the proverb for his last "fast day proclamation of his presidency." In his proclamation, he recommends a day of fasting and reflection to seek "God's pardoning mercy" so that the nation, as a whole, might be able to better pursue righteousness and turn away from sin.

People did not stop and wonder what was meant when biblical allusions were used in speeches by politicians or presidents. Newspaper writers did not use quotations to set off quotes from the Bible, because it was common knowledge.

And as we discussed previously, even folks who did not fully take the Bible's message to heart, like Thomas Jefferson or Benjamin

Franklin, still appealed to its principles because they knew the principles to be righteous and good. A person did not have to espouse the Christian faith in order to recognize the benefits to governance and order that the Bible provided. The Bible was not only part of the American lexicon; it continued to play a foundational role in early education.

## The Bible Was Central to Education

The early Puritan settlers knew that their children had to know the Bible. So they made sure the Bible was a focal point of their foundational curriculum. Benjamin Harris introduced *The New England Primer* (pronounced "prem-ur") to the people of Boston in 1690. This little book was taught to millions of children. They, and the Founding Fathers, learned to read by studying the *Primer* and the Bible. But the *Primer*, too, offered questions about the Bible and the Shorter Catechism as memory work.

To give you an idea of how central the Bible was to early education during the founding of our nation, here's an explanation of the value of learning the Shorter Catechism, found in the 1843 edition of the *Primer*:

> Our Puritan Fathers brought the Shorter Catechism with them across the ocean and laid it up on the same shelf with the family Bible. They taught it diligently to their children. . . . If in this Catechism the true and fundamental doctrines of the Gospel are expressed in few and better words and definitions than in any other summary, why ought we not now to train up a child in the way he should go?—why not now put him in possession of the richest treasure that ever human wisdom and industry accumulated to draw from.[2]

What is the Shorter Catechism that most young people learned during these early years of our nation? It's a short summary of the Christian faith, written in such a way as to benefit the reader as he or she memorizes its contents. It walks the reader through a series of questions and answers. Here are a few examples, taken from the 107 questions and answers given in the whole Shorter Catechism:

Q: What is the chief end of man?

A: Man's chief end is to glorify God and enjoy him forever.

Q: What do the scriptures principally teach?

A: The scriptures principally teach what man is to believe concerning God, and what duty God requireth of man.

Q: What is sin?

A: Sin is any want of conformity unto, or transgression of the law of God.

Q: What was the sin whereby our first parents fell from the estate wherein they were created?

A: The sin whereby our first parents fell from the estate wherein they were created, was their eating the forbidden fruit.

Q: Who is the Redeemer of God's elect?

A: The only Redeemer of God's elect, is the Lord Jesus Christ, who being the eternal Son of God, became man, and so was, and continues to be God and man, in two different natures, and one person forever.

Q: What is the sum of the ten commandments?

A: The sum of the ten commandments is, to love the Lord our God with all our heart, with all our soul, with all our strength, and with all our mind, and our neighbor as ourselves.

Q: What does every sin deserve?

A: Every sin deserves God's wrath and curse both in this life, and that which is to come.

**Q:** What does God require of us that we may escape his wrath and curse due to us for sin?

**A:** To escape the wrath and curse of God due to us for sin, God requireth of us faith in Jesus Christ, repentance unto life, with the diligent use of all outward means whereby Christ communicateth to us the benefits of redemption.

**Q:** What is faith in Jesus Christ?

**A:** Faith in Jesus Christ is a saving grace whereby we receive and rest upon him alone for salvation as he is offered to us in the gospel.[3]

Think of the influence this kind of education had upon the American family, on the culture at large, and on those who led our government. Think of the early institutions founded by various denominations. Of the first ten educational institutions in America, founded before 1776, only one was nonsectarian: the University of Pennsylvania (1751), commissioned by Benjamin Franklin. The rest were founded by the following denominations:

Harvard (1636)—Congregational
William and Mary (1693)—Episcopal
Yale (1701)—Congregational
Moravian (1742)—Moravian
Princeton (1746)—Presbyterian
Columbia (1754)—Episcopal
Brown (1764)—Baptist
Rutgers (1766)—Dutch Reformed
Dartmouth (1769)—Congregational

To gain entrance into Harvard College, students often lived with ministers who would privately tutor them until they had received sufficient training to take the entrance exam. Initially, Harvard existed to train men as clergy for service in their respective communities and churches. In the seventeenth and eighteenth centuries, the curriculum at Harvard focused on religion and Greek, Hebrew, and Latin. The presidents of Harvard in the seventeenth century were all clergy, and the sixth president, Increase Mather, focused the college on biblical ethics. The Bible saturated our nation's early educational vision.

## Put It In, Keep It Out

But some people did not want the Bible taught in schools, at least in the formative years of early education. Jefferson was one; his objections were similar to those encountered in the twentieth century. He wanted to shield young minds from "superstitions, fanaticisms, and fabrications taught by organized religions."[4] Jefferson believed that more mature minds (older youths) could better discern the "diamonds of Christ's ethical teachings."[5]

So there's nothing new under the sun. For hundreds of years, people have debated whether we should include the Bible in schools. Many argue now that it means whether the country separates church and state. But even Jefferson recognized the value in learning the moral and ethical principles of the Bible and did not oppose including it for older students.

The Bible stayed in schools throughout the nineteenth century. But slowly it disappeared from our curriculums. New advances in science and technology shifted curriculum toward the sciences. Languages like Greek, Hebrew, and Latin fell away, though now they are sometimes taught in some private schools and in homeschool curriculums.

As our attention shifted toward science, the Enlightenment flexed its muscle. Information and knowledge moved to the top of our lists.

Not only did the humanities move to the background of our educational focus, but the Bible all but vanished from the history books.

Think about it. Who teaches about the Bible's impact on our nation or on the world? Who looks at the Bible purely as a book that played a central part in the culture and thought behind our nation's founding?

## Keeping the Bible in the Conversation

Opposition in the face of the Bible has not curtailed its massive cultural influence the world over. Interestingly, even though the Bible continues to dominate global book sales and to emerge in the thoughts and even speeches of great leaders, the United States rarely includes it in high school curriculum as part of our national history, saying nothing of its role in world history.

Even atheist Richard Dawkins, long known for his incendiary rhetoric against organized religion, thinks young children should be taught about religion, just not indoctrinated. Dawkins says, "There is a value in teaching children about religion. You cannot really appreciate a lot of literature without knowing about religion. But we must not indoctrinate our children."[6]

Dawkins becomes more specific when he writes, "The King James Bible of 1611—the Authorized Version—includes passages of outstanding literary merit in its own right, for example the Song of Songs, and the sublime Ecclesiastes (which I am told is pretty good in the original Hebrew too). But the main reason the English Bible needs to be part of our education is that it is a major source book for literary culture."[7] Dawkins then notes over one hundred phrases that are commonly used today that come from the King James Version of the Bible.

You will regularly hear a news article in which you are told someone acted as a "good Samaritan." The story of the good Samaritan, of course, comes from the Bible, but if you don't know the Bible, you lose context for what is being reported. As Dawkins notes, there are countless references in literature to biblical ideas (for example, salt of the earth, an eye for an eye, my brother's keeper), but if you are not aware of the Bible, you are to some degree illiterate, unable to fully understand the meaning of those references.

Author and English professor Leland Ryken points out that when Martin Luther King Jr. said, "We will not be satisfied until justice rolls down like waters and righteousness like a mighty stream," he was invoking the words of Amos (Amos 5:24), a minor prophet found in the Old Testament.[8]

And what about some of the major works of Western literature?

Ryken points us to several titles that show the Bible's influence: *The Power and the Glory* by Graham Greene, *Measure for Measure* by William Shakespeare, *The Sun Also Rises* by Ernest Hemingway, *East of Eden* by John Steinbeck, *Absalom, Absalom!* by William Faulkner, *Evil under the Sun* by Agatha Christie, *Gilead* by Marilynne Robinson, and we could go on.

Though we part ways with Dawkins on much of what he says, we'd agree that children should be taught about the Bible.

Others agree about the value of teaching the Bible as it relates to studying the humanities. Though the United States Supreme Court, in the 1963 case *Abington v. Schempp*, outlawed mandatory Bible readings in public schools because it created an "establishment of religion," it did offer this important clarification on the matter of studying the Bible as a historic document: "It certainly may be said that the Bible is worthy of study for its literary and historic qualities. Nothing we have said here indicates that such study of the Bible or of religion, when presented objectively as part of a secular program of education, may not be effected consistently with the First Amendment."[9]

## Let's Give the Bible a Fair Shake

Like most people, we invite the dialogue with, learning from, and teaching of any book that has affected the world. Not to espouse its faith, if it claims one, but to learn from it objectively. Its proponents should engage leading scholars from around the world to research its history, tell its story, and show how it has affected the world, all being done objectively.

Think about what Theodore Roosevelt, our twenty-sixth president, said: "If a man is not familiar with the Bible, he has suffered a loss which he had better make all possible haste to correct."[10]

Don't get us wrong. We're not opposed to promoting our faith. We support many ministries with very clear objectives to spread their faith. But for the museum, it is all about the book. An example is the creation story.

The Bible begins with, "In the beginning God created the heavens and the earth" (Gen. 1:1). It also tells us in the book of Hebrews, "By faith we understand that the universe was formed at God's command" (Heb. 11:3). The Bible is honest and tells us that if we believe "God created," then we believe it by faith.

God did not prove it, and he never will.

If you are being honest, then you have to say that whatever you believe about the origin of the universe, you believe by faith. Science cannot prove origins any more than the Bible can. To state as a fact something that happened billions of years ago just can't be done.

For example, when Steve was touring the National Museum of Natural History, he took a picture of a sign that states, "Nearly 4.6 billion years ago . . . a star was born—our Sun." Likewise, the science textbook from the local public school states, "The solar system began to form about five billion years ago." These are statements of faith being made as fact. No one can state, with absolute certainty, what happened five billion years ago. It simply can't be done. We do not want to make these kinds of statements in the Bible museum.

So in the museum, we tell the narrative of the Bible: "In the beginning God created." But we never say, "*When* God created," because that would be making a statement of faith as fact.

In contrast, consider how many in the scholarly world routinely make strong statements not based on sourced facts but based solely on their own personal agenda. Anne Rice, the popular novelist and former atheist, made a striking observation. Here's what she discovered when she put her atheism to the test and dug deep into the scholarship that focused on who Jesus was as a historical figure:

> What gradually came clear to me was that many of the skeptical arguments—arguments that insisted most of the Gospels were suspect, for instance, or written too late to be eyewitness accounts—lacked coherence. They were not eloquent. Arguments about Jesus himself were full of conjecture. Some books were no more than assumptions piled on assumptions. Absurd conclusions were reached on the basis of little or no data at all.
>
> The whole case for the non-divine Jesus who stumbled into Jerusalem and somehow got crucified, that whole picture which had floated around the liberal circles that I frequented as an atheist for thirty years, that case was not made. Not only was it not made, I discovered in this field some of the worst and most biased scholarship I had ever read.[11]

We'll be the first to tell you about our faith. But we can't emphasize enough that we want the museum to be a place where we all come together to look at the Bible with open minds, without agendas. Some will say we want to use the museum as a stepping-stone to get the Bible into schools in order to fulfill our agenda. But we want it in schools because we honestly believe it belongs there. Not because of an agenda but because it's part of our heritage.

Growing up in Oklahoma, we and our fellow students were required by our public schools to take a class on Oklahoma history. We're sure many of you remember a similar requirement in your own state. If state governments think it necessary for all of us to possess a deeper knowledge of the state in which we reside, how much more should the federal government care about one of the major sources of inspiration during the founding of our nation? Whether you like the Bible or not, it should be taught in our schools.

Dr. Benjamin Rush was one of America's founders. He was very accomplished and one of the youngest signers of the Declaration of Independence. In a letter he wrote, he argues for teaching the Bible in schools:

> But passing by all other considerations, and contemplating merely the political institutions of the United States, I lament that we waste so much time and money in punishing crimes and take so little pains to prevent them. We profess to be republicans, and yet we neglect the only means of establishing and perpetuating our republican form of government; that is, the universal education of our youth in the principles of Christianity by means of the Bible; for this divine book, above all others, favors that equality among humankind, that respect for just laws, and all those sober and frugal virtues which constitute the soul of republicanism.[12]

We remember hearing a lecture given on the Bible's role in education during the time of our nation's founding. We sat astounded at our complete lack of knowledge regarding the Bible's prominence, not only in the lives of our country's founders but also in education. We both attended public schools, and through all of our schooling, we never heard the truth about the Bible's role in our country.

We felt cheated.

It was exciting to discover how the colonists, though never fully or perfectly, tried to build a nation on the principles of the Bible. Religious divisions abounded, but most leaders adhered to the idea that virtuous living should guide and direct our interactions. How incredible that the Bible was foundational to our nation's economy, governance, education, morality, and ultimately its success.

What does it mean to be a nation of the book? It will not mean a return to colonial America. That's obvious. But maybe it means setting down our agendas and considering the influence of a book that shaped a nation.

# CHAPTER 14

# THE ADVENTURE OF THE BIBLE

*In every instance where the findings of archaeology pertain to the Biblical record, the archaeological evidence confirms, sometimes in detailed fashion, the historical accuracy of Scripture. In those instances where the archaeological findings seem to be at variance with the Bible, the discrepancy lies with the archaeological evidence, i.e., improper interpretation, lack of evidence, etc.—not with the Bible.*

—DR. BRYANT C. WOOD, ARCHAEOLOGIST,
ASSOCIATES FOR BIBLICAL RESEARCH

*In the beginning was the Word, and the Word was with God, and the Word was God.*

—JOHN 1:1 ESV

*I know of no finding in archaeology that's properly confirmed which is in opposition to the Scriptures. The Bible is the most accurate history textbook the world has ever seen.*

—DR. CLIFFORD WILSON, FORMER DIRECTOR OF
THE AUSTRALIAN INSTITUTE OF ARCHAEOLOGY

No one likes to be told what to do. Especially when it comes to religion. We all dial into our personal beliefs, and that's that. Usually.

But how did we arrive at those beliefs? We learned the importance of striking a balance between holding on to the values our parents taught us and exploring a thing for ourselves. Our parents instilled fundamental life lessons and universal truths in us. We're thankful for our upbringing and feel blessed to have received it. But when it comes to personal faith, we believe people need to arrive there on their own. We shouldn't embrace something just because that's what we've been taught. We need to seek it out on our own and arrive at our own conclusions.

But there are some things all of us can be clueless about. We're all on a journey trying to figure this thing out. We don't have it all figured out, and we never will. We've learned to ask, "Do we really know enough about this to make a decision? Or are we simply relying on someone else's decision?"

We love the Bible because we've found it to be a book that invites exploration. Rodney Stark points out, in his excellent book *The Victory of Reason*, how the Christian faith invites exploration. Our family loves this aspect of the Bible. Scholars call Christianity a faith tradition that centers on orthodoxy.

Now, that word can scare people away. We get that, and we've been there. But Stark breaks *orthodoxy* down into two parts: *ortho*, meaning "correct," and *doxy*, meaning "opinion" or "belief." To believe something, a person must first take in the facts, observe, and dig a little. When they finish their exploration, they arrive at a conclusion. That conclusion takes the shape of a right belief—something explored, examined, and accepted.

## Exploring Truth

In the New Testament book of Acts, the writer, Luke, commends the Bereans because they didn't simply accept what Paul taught about Jesus. Rather they dug into the Scriptures themselves to discover whether Paul's teaching was accurate.

So the Bible commends exploration, to find out for ourselves who God is.

Personal exploration is important. For example, the Bible often does not spell out its principles in black and white. Gray issues exist. But rather than going with the cultural flow on gray areas, we should explore for ourselves and use our wisdom, discernment, and reason to decipher the best good for all.

Now, when we suggest that we should all do our best to explore God and the Bible for ourselves, that doesn't mean we will come up with different answers.

Arriving at right belief is like a complex math problem. You can solve it in different ways, but in the end you get the same answer. In our world, the idea that everyone can arrive at their own conclusion based on personal feelings about any given topic threatens the very way we think about truth.

If we all arrive at our own conclusions about murder based on how we feel on this day or that and depending on personal issues (like a relationship with the accused, and so on), how could we as a society ever make good laws governing violence and crime? It's reasonable, we believe, to say, "Yes, there are some beliefs basic to human existence." If we can't agree on universal truth, we can agree on nothing. And our chance at a reasonable society goes out the window.

There is, we believe, one truth. Not a truth for you and a truth for me.

Imagine if we applied subjective reasoning to the interpretation of the Bible. If this were a true method of interpretation, that would render the Bible's contents meaningless. We believe there are multiple applications for Scripture, but only one interpretation.

So when we come to the Bible seeking wisdom and spiritual health, we understand that the Bible instructs us with universal truth interpreted narrowly but applied broadly.

Earlier we shared about some struggles we encountered early in our marriage concerning debt. We encountered a radical new way to live: debt free. We took this knowledge and applied it to our personal lives. No longer ignorant of this truth, we lived in the peace it provided, and still do.

We took ownership of our faith. And explored, and discovered, a right belief on a topic mired in cultural nuance. We discovered that our faith was built on a relationship: us and God. We learned, through his Word (the Bible) and the advice of others, what the Bible refers to as wise counsel (Prov. 11:14). God wants us to seek him for ourselves. And when we do, the reward is the blessing of truth.

As we began this journey of acquiring biblical artifacts, we were like children learning to walk. The steps were elementary. We were like first-graders learning to read. We had no idea that there was an entire library of books waiting to be read and discovered.

## Museum Treasures

Part of our education about the world of biblical artifacts was learning the sheer number of them that existed. Not only that but also the variety of them. We've already referenced the Codex Climaci Rescriptus, in chapter 2. But there have been so many other discoveries along the way. Take a look for yourself.

*Gutenberg's Epistle to the Romans.* Gutenberg's printing press, with movable typeset, revolutionized printing. There were 35 copies of the Gutenberg Bible printed on vellum and 150 printed on paper; only 48 copies survived. Our collection contains what is called the noble fragment, consisting of Romans and the beginning of 1 Corinthians.

A Gutenburg Bible fragment containing the book of Romans, 1454. Johannes Gutenberg's first major printing project was the Latin Bible (Museum of the Bible).

*Elizabeth de Bohun, Book of Hours and Psalter.* This is one of the truly beautiful manuscripts in the collection. Elizabeth de Bohun was the countess of Northhampton (1313–56). She was one of the best-connected women in England and had a strong desire to patronize the arts. This book has truly wonderful and elaborate illustrations, worthy of any royalty. By the end of the nineteenth century, this book was owned by American aristrocrat John Jacob Astor, who loaned it to the Pedestal Art Loan Exhibition in 1883. This exhibition was held to raise money for the pedestal of the Statue of Liberty.[1]

The Book of Hours and Psalter of Elizabeth de Bohun, Countess of Northampton, a beautiful example of medieval illumination. This page, showing Psalm 1, features an illuminated initial B containing the Tree of Jesse (Museum of the Bible).

MOTB.MS.000761

*Esther Scroll.* While this is not one of the older items in our collection (circa 1900), it represents an interesting part of Jewish history. The Jewish holiday of Purim commemorates Esther, who rescued her Jewish brothers and sisters from a scheme by an official of the ruling Persian empire to destroy them. The Esther Scroll was read to the congregation as a memorial of those events. This exemplar was kept in an ornate silver case.

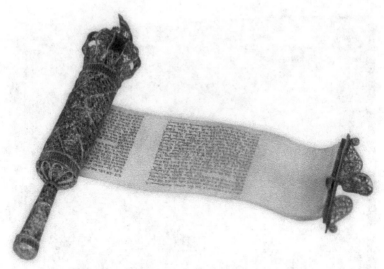

This exemplary Esther Scroll was kept in a silver scroll case measuring 20.2 centimeters in length and 5.5 centimeters in width (Green Collection).

GC.SCR.001971

*Aitken Bible, 1782.* During the Revolutionary War, all supplies from England were cut off to the colonies—including Bibles. Robert Aitken saw this as an opportunity and petitioned Congress to approve a Bible he was printing. In September 1782, Congress issued this resolution, which was printed in the front of the Bible: "Resolved: That the United States in Congress assembled highly approve the pious and laudable undertaking of Mr. Aitken . . . they [Congress] recommend this edition of the Bible to the inhabitants of the United States and hereby authorize him to publish this recommendation."

Aitken's Bible represents the only Bible ever approved by Congress. Congress promised ten thousand dollars to pay for the printing of thirty thousand copies but because of the financial constraints of the war never paid the bill.[2]

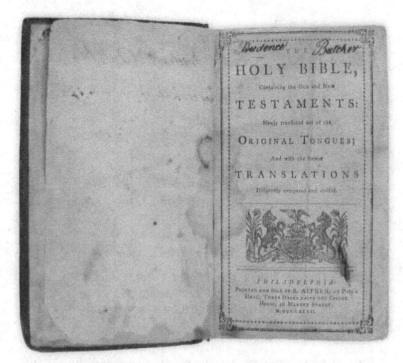

The 1782 Aitken Bible is the first English Bible printed in
America and was the only Bible ever approved by Congress.
Robert Aitken printed the congressional recommendation
in the first pages of his Bible (Green Collection).

GC.BIB.002615

*Bibles.* There are many and various Bibles from different peri-
ods and times. These Bibles include complete Bibles, excerpts, and
fragments. Some of the Bibles within the collection include a Paris
Pocket Bible, the Stephanus Bible (the first versified Latin Bible), a
Geneva Bible, a Tyndale New Testament, and a Martin Luther Old
Testament.

And it's not just the type of Bible but also the variety of language translations from around the world—whether Chinese,

Czech, Ge'ez, Icelandic, Swedish, or German. We found the number of American Indian translations equally interesting: Algonquin, Mohawk, Seneca, Dakota, Cherokee, and even the Ojibwa. There is even an Oregon Trail Bible.

The earliest Bible in a European language printed in North America was Christoph Saur's (1695–1758) edition of Luther's German Bible. Printed in Germantown, Pennsylvania, 1743 (Green Collection).

GC.BIB.001592

*An array of artifacts.* The greatest discovery for us, beyond Bibles, was the vast array and diversity of artifacts related to the Bible. These include things like Torah scrolls, letters, lectionaries, glossaries, prayer books, psalters, processional crosses, homilies, hymn books, printing blocks, commentaries, yads, menorahs, and even the works of John Bunyan. In the few pages of this book, we cannot begin to describe the depth and breadth of the artifacts in our collection, let alone those that exist around the world.

We've had one scholar describe our collection as simply awe-inspiring, and as you'll see, it was for us as well—in more ways than one.

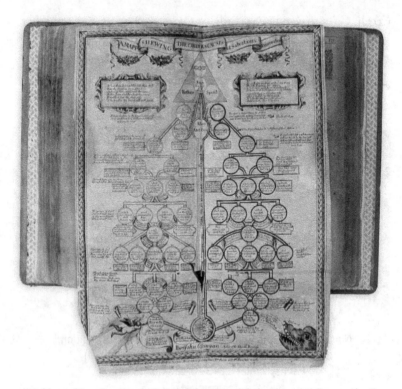

"A Mapp Shewing the Order and Causes of Salvation and Damnation"
from the works of John Bunyan, 1692 (Green Collection).

## The Fight for the Bible

When we look at the entire story of the Bible and how it came to be, we see that it's an amazing story. Here in the few pages of this chapter, we've attempted to describe some of that adventure. We've also sought to give you a picture of some of the history and the artifacts that make up the fabric of the book. Part of that journey are the men and women who leave their homeland, go to foreign lands, and undertake great feats because of a book. The writer of the book of Hebrews describes it dramatically:

THE ADVENTURE OF THE BIBLE

And what more shall I say? I do not have time to tell about Gideon, Barak, Samson and Jephthah, about David and Samuel and the prophets, who through faith conquered kingdoms, administered justice, and gained what was promised; who shut the mouths of lions, quenched the fury of the flames, and escaped the edge of the sword; whose weakness was turned to strength; and who became powerful in battle and routed foreign armies. Women received back their dead, raised to life again. There were others who were tortured, refusing to be released so that they might gain an even better resurrection. Some faced jeers and flogging, and even chains and imprisonment. They were put to death by stoning; they were sawed in two; they were killed by the sword. They went about in sheepskins and goatskins, destitute, persecuted and mistreated— the world was not worthy of them. They wandered in deserts and mountains, living in caves and in holes in the ground.

—HEBREWS 11:32–38

I'm not sure about you, but we find those words inspiring and challenging. There's something about a great quest that stirs the soul. We love heroes. We love underdogs.

Why?

Everyone wants to live a great adventure. We all want to have a life of meaning. That's the tricky part of the equation. With every great adventure, with every great quest, to make them interesting, there must be some opposition. The Bible talks about this. On the eve of his crucifixion, Jesus gathered his twelve closest friends in a room. He knew he was going to die, and you can imagine the sorrow hanging over the scene. As he prepared them for the future, he told them they would be put out of the synagogue—separated from their very own community. He told them plainly, "In this world you will have trouble" (John 16:33).

And that is our pause. There's an incredible story behind the Bible. There are parts of the story that read like a great novel. But there's a salty reality. There is opposition to the Bible. And there always will be. But there is a discovery worth making.

## Our Personal Discovery

We weren't looking for artifacts. We certainly were not looking to start a museum. Archaeology was not a subject we took in school. It was a word, at most, we'd heard and had a vague appreciation for.

In our personal lives, we'd read and appreciated the Bible text, but we simply had no idea of the artifact world surrounding the Bible. We've been blown away by all that we see. The efforts to preserve it. To translate it. To print it. To share it. To argue about it. To offer commentary. To meditate. To teach. To make beautiful illustrations. And to oppose it.

That depth and breadth of material surrounding the Bible has allowed our confidence to go deeper. There's a richness to our faith we could not have imagined as we see all the surrounding evidence.

We remain excited for the future because we believe that new discoveries lie ahead. There will be some great finds that provide new points of confirmation. There will be similarly new finds that will raise new questions, and we want to keep raising new questions, because that's part of the adventure.

# CHAPTER 15

# GODLY ARCHITECTURE: HOW THE BIBLE SHAPED OUR WORLD

*[Jesus] said to them, "Go into all the world and preach the gospel to all creation."*

—MARK 16:15

*It is impossible to rightly govern the world without God and the Bible.*

—GEORGE WASHINGTON

*Since the invention of printing, the Bible has become more than the translation of an ancient Oriental literature. It has not seemed a foreign book, and it has been the most available, familiar, and dependable source and arbiter of intellectual, moral, and spiritual ideals in the West.*

—H. GRADY DAVIS[1]

From where did most people believe humankind originated?

Charles Darwin died April 19, 1882. More than one hundred and thirty years later, his theory of evolution, based on the concept of natural selection and published as *The Origin of Species* in 1859, continues to influence the world. And not just in biology. In other fields of science and the humanities. But as much influence as Darwin continues to wield, it's interesting to ask, what did people believe about the origin of species before Darwin?

Most thought "humans were the pinnacle of godly architecture."[2] People, for centuries, believed the Bible's narrative, in which God creates humans so they can inhabit the world but also so he can commune with them. This fact is tough to consider in light of our modern world and the advancements of science and technology. But in reality, the idea that humans emerged from an evolutionary process based on random chance became popular only in the last few hundred years.

We find Charles Darwin listed among the one hundred most influential people in human history, according to *Time* magazine. But even though Darwin changed the course of science away from the long-standing, biblically influenced understanding of human origins, the list of influential people throughout history weighs heavy with "people of the book."

## A Beautiful Mosaic of People and Events That Shaped Our World

Though Darwin's book seems to shape our modern world, have we forgotten how deeply the Bible shaped our world for centuries prior? People talk about Darwin as if his work presents us with the ultimate truth about man's existence, when in reality it's nothing more than a theory.

Yet we, as a society, teach that theory in our schools as fact. How misleading is that to our children? Why not present young and old alike with more than one option. If we're going to teach theory, why not entertain the possibility of a loving God who created humankind to be in relationship with him.

Think about the great men and women throughout history who gave their lives to following God, reforming the church, explaining the universe, or translating the ancient texts into the common tongue. Do we simply focus on their acts apart from their faith?

If you stand back and look at the whole of history, it spreads out like a beautiful mosaic. Individual people acting and reacting, creating a succession of events—events that shape our world. In our information age, we've lost some of the appreciation for the past. We tend to focus so much on the immediate—the here and now. It's easy to forget the people and events that shaped our world, while we enjoy the conveniences of today.

For as much as we forget, *Time* magazine helps us remember.

In "The 100 Most Influential People of All Time," *Time* gives us a peek into those individuals whose lives have touched us all. In *History's Greatest Events: 100 Turning Points That Changed the World: An Illustrated Journey*,[3] *Time* opens up our eyes to the major events that shaped our world, chronicling more than 150 events, arranged from the ancient world to modern times.

From the ancient world, we meet Abraham (2100–1500 BC). He was the father of the Jewish nation and a key figure in the Hebrew Scriptures. Abraham represents both a history-shaping person and an event, as he turned away from a polytheistic world to a monotheistic world—from worship of many gods to worship of a singular god. Abraham's profound change of direction was "a revolution in thought. . . . [H]e changed religion, society and history."[4]

Next, *Time* introduces us to a list of characters who either are, like Abraham, characters from the Bible or were influenced by the Bible.

First, we meet Moses (1520–1400 BC). He was the great liberator of Israel from Egyptian slavery and perhaps an even greater biblical figure than Abraham. Moses talked with God and once boldly asked to see God's glory. In Exodus, the second book in the Torah, it says, "Thus the LORD used to speak to Moses face to face, as a man speaks to his friend" (Ex. 33:11 ESV).

Many years later, we run into Jesus of Nazareth (7–2 BC to AD 30–36). He was the son of a carpenter, a teacher, who became known as the Christ and is the primary figure of the Christian tradition. The authors note how "Christianity remains a central pillar of civilization, 20 centuries after Jesus . . . was crucified and, as his followers believe, rose from the dead and ascended to heaven."[5] We meet this carpenter's son in the second part of the modern Bible, known as the New Testament. The first four books, known as the Gospels, offer eyewitness accounts of his life and ministry. Jesus, as a historical figure the world over, remains one of the most controversial and influential figures ever in world history.

*Time* includes the apostle Paul (AD 5–67). Paul was from Tarsus—modern-day Turkey. He was a former religious leader, a self-described "Hebrew of Hebrews" (Phil. 3:5) who converted to Christianity following a supernatural encounter with Jesus after he was crucified and raised from the dead. Paul is also one of the main contributors to the New Testament.

Paul was instrumental in the proliferation of the first-century church, ministering to believers through letters and missionary journeys. As the church grew, it encountered major opposition in the form of persecution. We'll touch on this more in the final section, but one of the main characters responsible for helping the Christian tradition get on its cultural feet was Constantine (AD 280–337).

Constantine represents a key figure and marks a pivotal event in world history. He was the first Roman emperor to embrace Christianity. Constantine contributed to the spread of Christianity in a time when it was customary to follow the imperial cults of Rome. Two hundred years after the time of Jesus, people still considered Christianity a fringe cult and even believed that Christians ("little Christs"), as those in Antioch referred to them, participated in cannibalism. This rumor emerged from a misguided understanding of the Christian custom of sharing in the Eucharist, in which Christians drank wine and ate unleavened bread to symbolically remember Jesus' shed blood (wine) and broken body (bread).

Not only did Constantine expand his reach and defeat his barbarian enemies, but he embraced this new religion and allowed it to flourish.[6]

In Augustine of Hippo (AD 354–430), we go from king to saint. Augustine hailed from North Africa. He was a rambunctious young man and was fond of engaging in sexual exploits with women. But when he found religion in the Christian tradition, his conversion took him down a different path. He preached daily for thirty-five years and wrote one of the great works of Christian doctrine in *The City of God*. Augustine's thought and theological work continues to influence thinkers and theologians from both the Catholic and Protestant traditions.

As we leap forward a few hundred years into the medieval period, we find a kind monk who loved to be in nature. Saint Francis of Assisi

(AD 1182–1226) believed we are closest to God when we live in a place of want. This position was counter to the Catholic Church's push to be about industry. He was a humble man who valued the beauty of nature; at one point, Francis even preached to the birds.

As if a quiet humble monk who preached to birds isn't surprising enough as one considers the major influential people of history, we next discover the unlikely military success of a young woman who claimed she heard directly from God. Joan of Arc (AD 1412–1431) was a spiritual radical who played a vital role in leading France to overthrow English invaders. Some say that she's responsible for making France *want* to become a nation. Now, that's impact!

But every so often, a person comes along whose work undeniably changes the trajectory of human history. That person? Johannes Gutenberg (AD 1395–1468). His work? Printing the first Bible. Gutenberg was a German printer who adapted a winepress into a printing press in his journey to print the Bible for the very first time. Only an estimated forty-eight Gutenberg Bibles remain in existence today.

The spread of Christianity was further enhanced by Gutenberg. His printing press allowed books to be the world's first mass-produced items, and chief among those books was the Bible. This mass production allowed for the Age of Enlightenment to come to the common man and not just the socially elite.[7]

Looking down over our list, it almost seems like it is the humblest among us who make the biggest impact in history. But then we meet Martin Luther (AD 1483–1546). Martin Luther was the Catholic monk who initiated the Protestant Reformation and was a key figure in translating the Bible into the vernacular.

Luther was a lightning rod of controversy. After taking a trip to Rome from his monastery, he fumed at the Catholic Church's abuse of indulgences. In response, he wrote down his now (in)famous Ninety-Five Theses and nailed them to the church door. In Luther's time, however, this was not an act of vandalism. Rather it served as an invitation to discuss the grievances posted. The problem with Luther's grievances was that they were all grievances against the largest religious institution in the known world. That will get you in trouble every time.

Even as the common man gained the Bible, it was Luther's revolt against the Roman Catholic Church that stood equally tall. When Luther posted his Ninety-Five Theses on October 31, 1517, he could not have imagined the diversity of churches that would follow his efforts.[8]

Perhaps one thing can be easily overlooked: the work of Copernicus (AD 1473–1543). The Polish astronomer who reversed thirteen hundred years of scientific thought was also a man of religion, although the Catholic Church—his church—was not too happy about his astronomical views.

Up to the time of Copernicus, the common view was that the sun revolved around the earth. He, however, created a new thesis: the earth revolved around the sun.[9] His thesis served in part to help humankind realize they were not the center of the universe—a biblical concept.

Not surprisingly, his ideas were challenged, even by reformers like Martin Luther.[10] It wasn't until Galileo (1564–1642) that Copernicus's ideas were recognized for what they were—how a loving God could show favor to an insignificant world. Copernicus wrote, "[It is my] loving duty to seek the truth in all things, in so far as God has granted that to human reason."[11]

Up to this point in time, the center of religious activity was Europe. But as Europeans began to seek religious freedom, they set out for new lands. In 1620, the *Mayflower* made landfall in Massachusetts.[12] The new colonies began their own brand of Christian expansion, society, and culture.

While the New World expanded, Isaac Newton made a profound impact on the world of science. His *Principia Mathematica*, published in 1686, "put forth his theories of gravity and motion; it has been called the fundamental work for all of modern science."[13]

What few realize, since Newton's nonscientific writings were not published until 1936, is that Newton operated from a biblical worldview. "Newton's understanding of God came primarily from the Bible, which he studied for days and weeks at a time."[14] For Newton, the Bible and the idea of creation undergirded his science. It was not until much later that the war between science and religion would erupt, but not under Newton.[15]

As Newton created a new foundation for math and science, the New World began to emerge. As we've previously discussed, America was a country founded upon a unique set of ideals. A new era of expansion was launched in an altogether different kind of way.

In 1776, with America's Declaration of Independence, a country founded on biblical principles was a brand-new idea. As the authors of *History's Greatest Events* note, "Jefferson's assertion that all men 'are endowed by their Creator with certain unalienable rights, that among these are life, liberty and the pursuit of happiness' struck a chord in human hearts that has never stopped resounding. Those words became the rallying cry of French revolutionaries, of marchers who followed Mohandas Gandhi and Martin Luther King Jr., of Soviet dissidents, and Nelson Mandela, and, as of 2010, Tea-Party protesters. . . . A few words consigned centuries of hierarchies to history's dustbin."[16]

These ideas of the Creator endowing individuals with inalienable rights allowed America to take a great step forward at the time of the Civil War. President Lincoln noted in April 1861 that one-eighth of the population were slaves, with much of slavery localized in the South. The South sought to forward their interests in slavery, while the North sought to restrain it according to Lincoln.

He framed the Civil War conflict with the same principle Jefferson advocated: that all men are created equal. Lincoln's words still stir emotion: "Now we are engaged in a great Civil War, testing whether that nation, or any nation so conceived and so dedicated, can long endure."[17] The war of course ended slavery in America, and while our country's record on civil rights is imperfect, it was a step forward in the journey.

Though the Civil War marked the end of slavery in the United States, decades earlier we find a certain president waging his own war on slavery, in what might be considered a precursor to the abolition of slavery in America.

## John Quincy Adams and the *Amistad*

Few stories illustrate the impact of the Bible on the efforts to abolish slavery as that of the Mendi Africans, dramatized in the superb Steven Spielberg film *Amistad*.

In the film, it is 1839. American slavery is firmly entrenched in the South, and while opposed by many in the North, its tentacles are everywhere. Both sides are immovable in their convictions about the "good" and evil of slavery.

The Civil War won't break out for another two decades, but some are beginning to discuss the possibility of Southern secession and war. Some in the North openly call for secession from the South, believing that the Constitution, so long as it includes the South and the practice of slavery, is a pact with hell.

Meanwhile, in the South, people view northern efforts to restrict the spread of slavery as Yankee attempts at economic oppression of the South, both for their own profit and because of their disapproval of the "peculiar institution" of "property" that has become so integral to the Southern economy—namely, slavery.

In the midst of this increasingly lethal political powder keg, a Cuban ship named *Amistad* is seized off the coast of New York by the U.S. Navy. On board are Africans who were abducted from their homeland by Spanish planters but rebelled against their captors, killing the ship's captain and cook in the process.

The issue of what to do with the Africans is raised.

Should they be extradited to Cuba, a Spanish colony? Are they property?

Claims are filed by both the owner of the *Amistad* and the Spanish government. The case makes its way to the Supreme Court of the United States in 1841. President Martin Van Buren prefers to avoid a case that could have such an inflammatory impact on the slavery question and thus wants the Africans to be extradited to Cuba.

Abolitionists, on the other hand, have raised money to defend the Africans and their right to fight for their freedom against their captors. In their effort, they are able to recruit the now elderly John Quincy Adams to represent the Africans. The son of the American founder and second president John Adams, a former secretary of state, a former president of the United States, a current congressman, and a lifelong opponent of slavery, John Quincy Adams argues that the Africans, as men, were as justly entitled to fight for their freedom against their captors as any other.

While in prison, the Africans are exposed to the Bible and converted to Christianity. They have found a champion in Jesus, who was also a good and righteous man, unjustly tortured and executed.

In a letter to Adams written before he argues before the Supreme Court, one of the Africans writes to him that "wicked people want to make us slaves but the great God who has made all things raise up friends for Mendi people he give us Mr. Adams that he may make me free and all Mendi people free."

Another expresses his hope that "the great God will send down His Holy Spirit upon you and have mercy upon you and that our dear savior Jesus Christ will bless you."[18]

Their prayers are seemingly answered.

Citing the Declaration of Independence and the Bible, among other authorities, Adams wins the case, and the Supreme Court rules in favor of the Africans, who are freed and returned to Africa.

Adams' efforts against slavery, both in the *Amistad* case and throughout his life, were no doubt partly inspired by his love of the Bible. In his concluding remarks to the Supreme Court, he cited the words of Jesus as he expressed his desire that the justices "may, every one, after the close of a long and virtuous career in this world, be received at the portals of the next with the approving sentence—'Well done, thou good and faithful servant; enter thou into the joy of thy Lord' [Matt. 25:21 KJV]."[19]

Clearly, Adams knew that the *Amistad* case was more significant than most court cases, for it went to the core issue of human dignity, and he wanted the justices to be aware of their eternal destiny before the final Judge (God) as they made their decision.

Out of gratitude, the Africans gave Adams a gift—none other than a Bible, which had inspired them in prison, and which they knew inspired him as well. They wrote the following in a letter presenting the Bible to him:

Most Respected Sir,

The Mendi people give thanks for all your kindness to them. They will never forget your defense of their rights before the great court at Washington [the Supreme Court of the United States]. They feel that they owe to you, in a large measure, their deliverance from the Spaniards, and from slavery or death. They will pray for you as long as you live, Mr. Adams.

May God bless and reward you. We are about to go home to Africa. We go to Sierra Leone first, and then we reach Mendi very quick. When we get to Mendi, we will tell the people of your great kindness. Good missionary will go with us. We shall take the Bible with us. It has been a precious book in prison, and we love to read it now we are free!

Mr. Adams, we want to make you a present of a beautiful Bible! Will you please to accept it, and when you look at it, or read it, remember your poor and grateful clients!

We read in this holy book, "If it had not been the Lord who was on our side, when men rose up against us, then they had swallowed us up quick, when their wrath was kindled against us. Blessed be the Lord, who hath not given us a prey to their teeth.

Our soul is escaped as a bird out of the snare of the fowler; the snare is broken and we are escaped. Our help is in the name of the Lord, who made Heaven and Earth" [Ps. 124].

For the Mendi people,<br>Cinque, Kinna, Kale[20]

In responding to their gift, Adams both thanked them and affirmed the Bible's role in inspiring his work on their behalf:

My Friends—

I have received the elegant Bible, which you have presented to me. . . . I accept it, and shall keep it as a kind remembrancer [sic] from you, to the end of my life.

It was from that book that I learnt [sic] to espouse your cause when you were in trouble, and to give thanks to God for your deliverance. . . . [T]ell your countrymen of the blessings of the book which you have given to me.

May the Almighty Power who has preserved and sustained you hitherto, still go with you, and turn to your good, and to that of your country, all that you have suffered, and all that may hereafter befall you.[21]

These words, written by an elderly Adams, were perfectly in line with sentiments he had expressed decades earlier to his young son: "[S]o great is my veneration for the Bible, and so strong my belief, that when duly read and meditated on, it is of all books in the world that which contributes most to make men good, wise, and happy."[22]

For Adams, the Bible was a book which, above all others, taught men to be good and just. Clearly, these were no idle thoughts. Just ask the Mendi Africans.

## And What Shall We Say Then?

These are but a thimbleful of the events in our world that have been driven or influenced by the Bible or the teachings of the Bible. In fact, the events listed here are those compiled by *Time* as they simply tried to describe 152 turning points in history. These don't even begin to encompass the countless events that have occurred in art, science, music, literature, business, fashion, government, and everyday life that have been impacted by the Bible.

It's worth noting that at the Museum of the Bible, we have an entire floor dedicated to the impact of the Bible on the world. Even there, we attempt to provide merely a sampling of the Bible's impact on the world throughout time. The entire floor isn't enough to demonstrate its impact on every facet of life.

There's a key subtext when we talk about the Bible's impact. The principles contained in this book can be applied by anyone, whether they declare themselves Christian or not. We've seen, from the narrative above, the fight for equality and how it emanates from the basic biblical idea of equality, and that theme has pounded like a drumbeat throughout the whole of human history. We see that when those principles are applied—again, whether by Christians or not—that the principles yield good fruit.

Indeed, biblical principles of love, fidelity, honesty, truth, hard work, and faithfulness are ideas that ring universal. To the contrary, the ideas of hatred, anger, jealousy, and greed yield an often disastrous result. Some question the stories of the Bible, yet they tell of an imperfect people working out these big ideas. We've seen the impact of the Bible in our own imperfect lives. We keep working out these noble principles day by day. And with it all, we ask ourselves a simple question:

What would the world be like without the Bible?

# PART 5

# TO THE ENDS OF THE EARTH

## ἀλλὰ λήμψεσθε δύναμιν

*"You will receive power when the Holy Spirit comes on you; and you will be my witnesses in Jerusalem, and in all Judea and Samaria, and to the ends of the earth."*

—ACTS 1:8

*Wouldn't we be happy if we could find the full treasure described in the Gospel?*

—BROTHER LAWRENCE, *THE PRACTICE OF THE PRESENCE OF GOD*

CHAPTER 16

# THE OPPOSITION

*"If the world hates you, keep in mind that it hated me first."*

—JOHN 15:18

*To be fair, much of the Bible is not systematically evil but just plain weird, as you would expect of a chaotically cobbled-together anthology of disjointed documents, composed, revised, translated, distorted and "improved" by hundreds of anonymous authors, editors and copyists, unknown to us and mostly unknown to each other, spanning nine centuries.*

—RICHARD DAWKINS, *THE GOD DELUSION*

*The Lord gave you a mind that you would make honest use of it. I'm saying you must be sure that the doubts and questions are your own, not, so to speak, the mustache and walking stick that happen to be the fashion of any particular moment.*

—MARILYNNE ROBINSON, *GILEAD*

Jesus left this world with a bang. Not literally. But three of the Gospels record him meeting with various people after he rose from the dead. For forty days he walked the earth, post-resurrection. Then he walked out to a place near Bethesda and ascended into heaven. Some recognize, and celebrate, this as Ascension Day.

But before he ascended, he charged his disciples with a task: take my message—the good news—to the ends of the earth and baptize people in the name of the Father, Son, and Holy Spirit. And then he was gone.

The disciples left worshiping God and praising his name. This command, as we have pointed out, is called the Great Commission. It came from Jesus and acted as a precursor to the church. At that point, Jesus' disciples were more localized.

But when Jesus left, the message went forth in all the nearby areas and far-off nations, thanks in part to the Roman road system and the long years of peace in the land known as the *Pax Romana* ("Roman peace") that extended into the second century. Tag on to those remarkable cultural realities the common language of Greek—thanks to Alexander the Great's conquests—and you have the perfect time for Jesus' message to appear on the scene and disseminate. Some theologians say this is what the apostle Paul meant when he said, "When the fullness of time had come, God sent forth his Son" (Gal. 4:4 ESV).

The message went out through Jesus' disciples, including the apostle Paul, whose letters to the early Christian gatherings, known as churches, circulated as a way to instruct and encourage the followers of Jesus in their newfound faith. But though the message of Jesus spread far and wide and with uncommon speed, it did find opposition. When we read the Acts of the Apostles (commonly known as the book of Acts), we read how Paul was beaten and imprisoned and seemed to carry out his ministry responsibilities under constant threat.

Jesus, however, did not send his disciples out as sheep to the cultural slaughter. He told them, "If the world hates you, keep in mind that it hated me first" (John 15:18). He told them to expect trials and tribulation, to expect persecution. But he also told them that he would be with them.

Yet despite persecution and the threat of death, the message of Jesus endured.

## Heroes of the Faith

Heroes thrive on opposition. It makes for a good story. It also makes for dynamic characterization. We like a good battle. We enjoy watching a struggle. Tension is good.

The Bible knows opposition. It may be your hero. It may not be. Either way, its pathway to existence winds through enemy camps. And its continued staying power shines even in the face of government bans and public burnings.

It is a book loved and maligned. One has only to look at its cultural birthplace to understand how much opposition the Bible had to overcome on the road to being the world's most known book.

It's important, however, to consider the "people of the book" as well—the Christians, as they were called. It was the early Christians who circulated its texts, including the books we now call the Old Testament, along with the early copies of the gospel accounts of Jesus' life, and the many letters that make up the remaining parts of what we now call the New Testament. The early Christians faced massive opposition in the form of martyrdom. Wave upon wave of persecutions beat down on those early adherents to this rogue faith.

Today we can read all about these persecutions in *Foxe's Book of Martyrs*.[1] This book details the sufferings of the early Christians and their consistent persecutions throughout ancient times until the middle of the first millennium.

The author, John Foxe, born in 1517 in Boston, England, just at the dawn of the Protestant Reformation, was educated at Oxford University. In 1563, he wrote *The Acts and Monuments*, a detailed history of Christian persecution. We know this book now as *Foxe's Book of Martyrs*. It's a work so influential that "after the Bible itself, no book so profoundly influenced early Protestant sentiment."[2]

We read, for example, about Nero, the sixth emperor of Rome. On a whim, he ordered the city of Rome set on fire while he played a harp and sang of the burning of Troy. The great fire lasted nine days. When he discovered that people blamed him for the destruction, he blamed the Christians and began to persecute them with violent aggression. *Foxe's Book of Martyrs* records how Nero "had some [Christians] sewed up in skins of wild beasts, and then worried by dogs until they expired; and others dressed in shirts made stiff with wax, fixed to axletrees, and set on fire in his gardens, in order to illuminate them."

Early church theologian Tertullian famously said, "The blood of the martyrs is the seed of the Church." What did he mean by this? Some think the early Christian church grew because of persecution. New studies suggest that many factors contributed to the spread of Christianity.[3] One thing appears certain. Opposition to the Christian faith galvanized people who followed Jesus. And just as Christians faced and continue to face hostility in many parts of the world, so did their holy book.

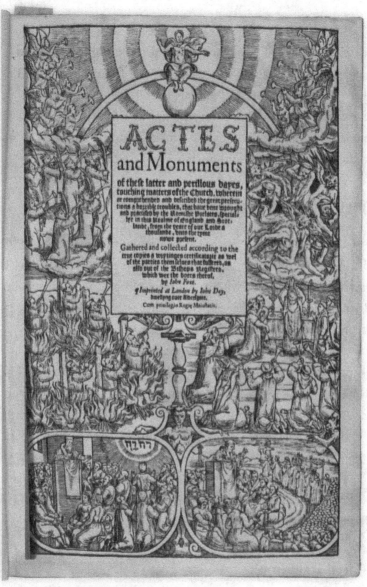

A first edition of John Foxe's *Actes and Monuments*, one of the most influential English works ever printed. The book was produced and illustrated
with fifty woodcuts and numerous four- to six-line decorated and historiated
initials executed by German artists. It was the largest and most complicated
publishing project in England to that time (Museum of the Bible).

In America, we enjoy freedom of religion, so in some respects it feels odd to think about such harsh persecutions. The Bible is so accepted that it's hard to think about it ever facing opposition. But that's the wonder of it. And the danger of it. Before all the accessible translations, before all the various ways we can access it thanks to modern technology, the Bible faced an uphill battle. One that began in the birthplace of the faith itself.

## Destroying the Bible's Home

Jerusalem was destroyed twice. The Babylonians destroyed it in 586/7 BC. They destroyed everything, including the famed Jerusalem wall and Solomon's Temple, with its beautiful artwork. What they didn't destroy, they looted. The Old Testament book of 2 Kings 25:8–21 records a list of the items taken by the intruders.

And yet the ancient texts endured. We find Jesus himself, for example, reading from the scroll of Isaiah, as recorded in the New Testament (Luke 4:17–21). Not long after Jesus' death and resurrection, the Romans destroyed Jerusalem. In AD 70, they burned the temple. The Torah and books of prophecy would have been stored there.

Yet despite the violent opposition of Syrian-Greek, Babylonian, and Roman empires, the Scriptures that would become the Old Testament of the Bible endured.

## Illegal Holy Books

It's easy to jump from the destruction of Jerusalem in AD 70 to the reign of Constantine, the Roman emperor responsible for making the religion of Christianity legal in AD 313 in the proclamation known as the Edict of Milan. Constantine was a major figure in the history of the church. The Christian faith found great favor during his rule. But he was far from biased toward Christianity.

As the story goes, Constantine had invaded Italy on his way to Rome. Here he faced a stout enemy in Maxentius. Maxentius relied on pagan magic for his tactical power. When Constantine heard of this, he felt he needed a more powerful force. One afternoon while he was praying, he had a vision. Church historian Kenneth Scott Latourette describes the vision as being "of a cross of light in the heavens bearing the inscription, 'Conquer by this,' and that confirmation came in a dream in which God appeared to him with the same sign and commanded him to make a likeness of it and use it as a safeguard in all encounters with his enemies."[4]

So Constantine fashioned a spear like the one from his dream. It was "overlaid with gold with a cross which was formed by a transverse bar and a wreath of gold and precious stones enclosing a monogram of the letters Chi and Rho for the name of Christ."[5] Constantine eventually triumphed over Maxentius at the battle of Milivian Bridge near Rome.

It was after this key battle that Constantine met with Licinius, who shared control of the realm with him, and issued a letter of declaration of toleration for Christians. But Constantine did not outlaw paganism in favor of Christianity. Rather he backed both. He held the title *pontifex maximus* throughout his reign, which designated him chief priest of the pagan state cult.

It would be easy to argue for preservation of biblical texts beyond his reign. But before Christianity became sanctioned by the state, thanks to Constantine, it was outlawed along with its books. Roman authorities banned Christian books. They refused them circulation, and when found, confiscated them or burned them.

Just before the reign of Constantine, between AD 303 and 311, Roman emperors Galerius and Diocletian waged a war on Christianity.

We know this time today as the Great Persecution. Authorities burned Christians alive and fed them to lions in the colosseum for sport. And "Roman officials began systematically confiscating and burning 'Christian Scripture.'"[6]

One rather funny anecdote to the authorities' burning of Scripture is the fact that the officers charged with executing the orders of the emperor could not tell a Bible from any other book. So when the officers came to Mensurius, a fourth-century bishop in Carthage, he gave them his collection of writings from heretics, while keeping his copies of the Scriptures safely out of the way.

So even though adherents to the relatively new religion of Christianity faced extreme persecution, and their collection of Holy Scriptures was at risk, the faith grew. Some historians suggest that the persecutions fueled Christianity's growth.[7] But as Christianity grew in Europe in the fourth century, it faced an uphill battle in Africa and Asia.

In Europe, the Bible was relatively central to political and religious life. However, the common person's lack of access to Scripture in Europe, especially after printed books became more readily available, can be seen as a kind of opposition. Over time, this opposition would be remedied by early Bible translators such as John Wycliffe and William Tyndale.

In the meantime, however, the Catholic Church ensured the Bible's influence as it preserved, copied, and passed down the Scriptures for the next ten centuries. This work was encouraged in Europe, as authorities did not actively seek to destroy the Scriptures, as in other parts of Asia and Africa.[8]

## Crisis of Two Books

What was it about Asia and Africa that created so much opposition to the Bible?

Some suggest the rise of other religions, such as Islam. By the seventh century, the Qur'an changed the religious landscape entirely, presenting a crisis of two books. On the one side, the Bible and its missionaries continued to swell in number of followers. On the other side, the Qur'an swept through the Arab world, eating up the ground previously claimed by the Bible and Christianity.

Muhammad himself, it seems, was influenced by Christianity, which may be the reason why he addresses Christianity in the Qur'an. "However and whatever Muhammad learned about Christianity," writes historian Derek Cooper, "the Qur'an leveled a thorough critique of the Christian religion, though it also required Muslim leaders to protect Christians under their jurisdiction."[9]

But even as the Bible faced opposition then, it's not as if missionaries just packed up shop, took their Bibles, and headed home. In the Bible, God, through the prophet Isaiah, reminds readers that his Word does not return to him void. It carries out its assignment. So today, though certain parts of the world, such as the Middle East and Asia, seem dominated by religions such as Islam, Judaism, Hinduism, and Buddhism, the Bible maintains a presence in form through staunch followers working to spread its message.

## The Common Man's Bible

So how did the Bible become part of the common person's library?

Although Christianity had a strong foothold in Europe since the days of the Roman Empire, European reformers from the twelfth century through the Reformation led movements that emphasized the importance of Christians actually reading the Bible. These movements occurred under the umbrella of Catholicism.

Peter Waldo's Waldensians "emphasized preaching, Bible study, laity and vernacular translations" in the twelfth century. The fourteenth-century Modern Devotion movement focused on, among other reforms, "Scripture reading, and solitude."

John Wycliffe rejected the ideas of exclusively Latin liturgies and Bibles. He died before he could be declared a heretic, but he was able to begin translating the Bible before his death.[10] He believed that priests and bishops should understand and teach from the Bible, but he also believed that you didn't need to be a person of letters to read and understand the Bible for yourself.

Martin Luther's reformation was the culmination of Luther's own forceful beliefs and the work of early reformers, like Wycliffe. Luther also worked tirelessly to translate the Bible into the common German tongue. After Luther's now-famous trial at the Diet of Worms in 1521, in which Luther was placed under the imperial ban, Frederick the Wise "had Luther hidden away for safekeeping in the castle at Wartburg."[11] There Luther spent his time in solitude, translating Erasmus's Latin New Testament into German. It took him only a remarkable eleven weeks!

It took renegades like Wycliffe and Luther to barrel ahead, fight the system, and provide the everyman with his own copy of the Bible in his own heart language. Their efforts ring out in our culture. Ever wonder why nearly every hotel room in the U.S. has a Gideon Bible? We have Wycliffe, Luther, and Tyndale before them, among others, to thank for the notion that everyone deserves access to the Bible.

Widespread personal access to the Bible was a hard-won battle, fought for hundreds of years. A notable movement inspired by the Reformation was Pietism. There was Reformed Pietism, Lutheran Pietism, and Moravian Pietism. Pietism was just as influential— perhaps even more so—as Puritanism in the early founding of America. It stressed personal conversion, holiness of life (or righteous living), and, most notably, Bible reading and prayer, along with spiritual reflection.[12]

American Puritanism and Pietism go hand in hand in their focus on Bible reading. Puritans and Pietists were a God-obsessed people whose love for Bible reading can best be encapsulated by the Puritan preacher Thomas Watson: "Leave not off reading the Bible till you find your heart warmed. . . . Let it not only inform you, let it inflame you."[13]

Christian reformation in Europe was often brutal. The church itself suffered divisions, and many people became martyrs. However, the common man gained much more access to Scripture.

## The Burning Bible

Today the Bible is still attacked. The attacks in America may not cost a person their life, but the attacks are real. They usually come in one of several forms. People argue that the Bible is not true or not good. We can't provide evidence for all of the Bible, but time and time again the evidence has shown the Bible to be accurate. As the argument goes, an absence of evidence is not evidence of absence. Or the second argument is that the Bible has been bad for society. The examples cited include the Crusades, the Spanish Inquisition, and slavery. While there are these and plenty of other examples, as we have stated, you shouldn't blame the Bible for man's misuse of it.

Another argument that is used today is science. Supposedly, to believe in the Bible is to disbelieve science. I (Steve) suspect that most do not know that it was a belief in the God of the Bible that led to much of the science we have today.

Then there are the outspoken atheists who have become very vocal in their atheism—some from their position as professors, some through media outlets, and some by writing books that have become bestsellers. These people have become very bold in espousing their faith, that there is no God.

Then there are those who, without having read the Bible, automatically reject any reference to the book. They attack and turn off those taking a position from or for the Bible.

While the rhetoric has become louder, Americans still have access to the Bible and can easily forget that the Bible is still being banned and burned in other parts of the world.

In Burma, hostile government police forces "reportedly burned sixteen thousand Bibles printed in ethnic languages"[14] in a single year. In North Korea, simply owning a Bible is enough to justify the owner's execution.[15] There are reports that a couple found reading the Bible in Iran were subject to torture and threatened that, were they found studying the Scriptures again, the authorities would take custody of their young daughter.[16] The same words that decorate walls and lie on coffee tables in some countries are considered criminal in others.

The Bible is burned figuratively as well. It is demeaned and discredited on a daily basis in every country in the world. In efforts to discredit the Bible's central figure, Jesus, and its message, opponents of God and the Bible believe that all they must do is demonstrate how rife the Bible is with contradiction and inconsistencies.[17] It's a credibility attack. The bold claims set forth in the Bible lose their credibility if it's all based on contradiction.

If skeptics don't attack contradictions, they marginalize belief in God by pitting it against something like science or our own minds and hearts. Bertrand Russell, in his essay "Why I Am Not a Christian," says, "Science can teach us, and I think our hearts can teach us, no longer to look around for imaginary supporters, no longer to invent allies in the sky, but rather to look to our own efforts here below to make the world a fit place to live."[18]

Or, like the famed late atheist Christopher Hitchens, they make provocative statements that ruthlessly attempt to shred every ounce of the Bible's credibility: "The Bible may, indeed does, contain a warrant for trafficking in humans, for ethnic cleansing, for slavery, for bride-price, and for indiscriminate massacre, but we are not bound by any of it because it was put together by crude, uncultured human mammals."[19]

For "people of the book," like us, one approach to defending the Bible is simply following its message to love God and love others. The apostle Peter, one of Jesus' closest friends and disciples, wrote this to first-century Christians: "If with heart and soul you're doing good, do you think you can be stopped? Even if you suffer for it, you're still better off. Don't give the opposition a second thought. Through thick and thin, keep your hearts at attention, in adoration before Christ, your Master. Be ready to speak up and tell anyone who asks why you're living the way you are, and always with the utmost courtesy" (1 Peter 3:15 MSG).

In the New Testament, as we said earlier, Jesus spoke to his followers about opposition. He told them to expect it. And he was right. History, as we've seen, fills up quickly with opposition to the Bible and its followers. And yet the Bible continues to flourish, not only as a book read by billions of people but also as a guide for life in this world of ours.

For those who embrace the Bible as their guidebook, it is hard to imagine how we would live without it. It's not uncommon to hear a Bible follower state something like, "I don't know how I would get through difficult times in life without it, and I'm thankful I don't have to."

One might argue that the Bible has faced opposition through the years because of its bold claims. And yet it continues to maintain its high-record sales. People continue to be martyred for their belief in its claims. What other book can elicit such a following, such a response, such passion, such misunderstanding, such beautiful acts, such wonder?

# CHAPTER 17

# WHAT HAS BEEN SAID ABOUT THIS AMAZING BOOK

*All Scripture is God-breathed and is useful for teaching, rebuking, correcting and training in righteousness, so that the servant of God may be thoroughly equipped for every good work.*

—2 TIMOTHY 3:16–17

*In matters not explicitly addressed by the Bible, it implies that what is true and right and beautiful is to be assessed by criteria consistent with the teachings of scripture. All of this implies that the Bible has final authority over every area of our lives and that we should, therefore, bring all our thinking and feeling and acting into line with what the Bible teaches.*

—JOHN PIPER, *A PECULIAR GLORY*

*"Isn't God good," Deena said. It was a declaration, not a question. Sam smiled and nodded his head in agreement. God is good, he thought. Bewildering, but good.*

—PHILIP GULLEY, *JUST SHY OF HARMONY*

In 2013, a new miniseries ran on cable TV's History Channel. It was the most watched entertainment program of the entire year on cable. The name of the program?

*The Bible.*

Over 13 million viewers tuned in for the series debut. Each week, viewership increased by 14 percent as the miniseries averaged 11.7 million viewers. So people in America find the Bible interesting.[1]

That same year, evangelical faith and culture research group Barna ran a study asking what people thought about the Bible. Though this represents a mere snapshot in our ever-changing society, with these statistics changing every year, let's look at a few highlights from the study to get a bead on what people think about the Bible in the twenty-first century.

They discovered that 80 percent of Americans consider the Bible to be holy. Fifty-six percent of Americans believe the Bible has too *little* influence in today's society. Thirty-one percent of Americans admitted their faith influences their voting "a great deal." People who read the Bible are more likely to give to charity. Forty-seven percent strongly agree that the Bible contains everything a person needs to know to live a meaningful life. Seventy-four percent of Bible readers strongly agree that reading the Bible makes a person more thankful. What were people's favorite book of the Bible? Psalms, by a long shot. Have we gone totally digital in our Bible reading preference? No doubt this number continues to change, but in 2013, nine out of ten people preferred a hard copy of the Bible over a digital copy.[2]

## What the Bible Says about Itself

The Bible makes some very bold claims.

First, it says it is the Word of God. In the Old Testament book of Nehemiah, chapter 8, we're told the law of Moses was read, and in verse 8 it claims it is the law of God. In the book of Joshua, it says, "Joshua said to the Israelites, 'Come here and listen to the words of the LORD your God'" (Josh. 3:9).

Sticking with the Old Testament, in Jeremiah 36 we read that Jeremiah dictated the "words of the LORD" (v. 6), and after the king threw the scroll they were written on into the fire, Jeremiah again dictated the "words of the LORD."

David, the writer of Psalm 1, writes this interesting promise:

> Blessed is the one
> who does not walk in step with the wicked
> or stand in the way that sinners take
> or sit in the company of mockers,
> but whose delight is in the law of the LORD,
> and who meditates on his law day and night.
> That person is like a tree planted by streams of water,
> which yields its fruit in season
> and whose leaf does not wither—
> whatever they do prospers.
>
> —PSALM 1:1–3

To claim that "whatever they do prospers" is a bold promise in and of itself, but notice it is for those who delight in the "law of the LORD." You could argue that the writer is specifically speaking of the law of Moses, which is, as we previously noted, the first five books of the Bible. But we believe that the phrase has a larger meaning and that it applies to the Bible as a whole.

Second, the Bible claims that it is going to last forever; it is literally unchanging. In Psalm 119, it says, "Forever, O LORD, your word is firmly fixed in the heavens" (v. 89 ESV); in Isaiah 40, it says, "The grass withers, the flower fades, but the word of our God will stand forever" (v. 8 ESV); and in Luke 21, Jesus says, "Heaven and earth will pass away, but my words will not pass away" (v. 33 ESV).

Imagine making either of these claims today. You write something and claim that it is God's Word or that it will last forever, and see what kind of response you get. Yet the Bible claims just that.

In the apostle Peter's second letter, he makes the claim that God inspired the writers of the Bible through the Holy Spirit. Peter writes, "No prophecy of Scripture comes from someone's own interpretation. For no prophecy was ever produced by the will of man, but men spoke from God as they were carried along by the Holy Spirit" (2 Peter 1:20–21 ESV).

The apostle Paul agrees: "Every scripture inspired of God is also profitable for teaching, for reproof, for correction, for instruction which is in righteousness" (2 Tim. 3:16 ASV). In the New International Version, that same passage reads, "All Scripture is God-breathed," which is another way to say it is inspired by God himself. That's a pretty hefty statement.

Another claim, which may be the most outrageous, comes to us from the fourth chapter of Hebrews, where it says the Word of God is "living and active" (v. 12 ESV). That's an incredible claim. It's a book. How can you say it is living? The German reformer Martin

Luther writes, "The Bible is alive, it speaks to me; it has feet, it runs after me; it has hands, it lays hold of me."[3] How can a book make such an outrageous claim and be taken seriously, much less become the bestselling book of all time? These simple facts make it more intriguing and worthy of being studied.

What is its history?

How did we get it?

Who wrote it?

Is it true or a fairy tale?

What impact has it had?

Why has this book had the impact it has?

What story does the book tell?

There are many who maintain strong feelings about this book. It is loved and it is hated. Over time, people have died defending it, and there are those who have hated it enough to kill those defending it. How could a book, and the beliefs and faith associated with the book, incite this much devotion and hatred, all at the same time? What does that say about the human condition? Could it be that the Bible helps us understand our condition and the internal struggle for meaning and purpose?

Whether you love it or hate it, it is worth your time to get to know it. And many great thinkers and leaders throughout history have done so.

## Historical Buzz about the Bible

So much has been said and written about the Bible throughout history. But if we take the time to survey the comments of a few people who valued the Bible, we can more clearly see the enduring and esteemed view of the Bible and understand how it seems to be the thread connecting so many world leaders and brilliant minds.

Augustine of Hippo wrote the famous *City of God* and *Confessions*. He's regarded as one of Christianity's most brilliant theological minds, embraced by Protestants and Catholics alike. In his intimate, journal-like book *Confessions,* he writes of his youthful disdain of the Bible yet notes how the Bible grows along with the reader, if the reader is open to it: "My inflated conceit shunned the Bible's restraint, and my gaze never penetrated to its inwardness. Yet the Bible was composed in such a way that as beginners mature, its meaning grows with them. I disdained to be a little beginner. Puffed up with pride, I considered myself a mature adult."[4]

Abraham Lincoln requires little introduction. Lincoln was known for not only using Scripture adeptly in discourse but also studying the Bible. In a reply to an African American organization in Baltimore upon presentation of a Bible on September 7, 1864, Lincoln wrote, "In regard to this Great Book, I have but to say, it is the best gift God has given to man. All the good the Savior gave to the world was communicated through this book. But for it we could not know right from wrong. All things most desirable for man's welfare, here and hereafter, are to be found portrayed in it."[5]

In an essay, Victor Hugo, the Romantic French novelist and poet who wrote the towering *Les Misérables*, writes, "The Bible, Homer, hurt us sometimes by their very sublimities. Who would want to part with a word of either of them? Our infirmity often takes fright at the inspired bold flights of genius, for lack of power to swoop down upon objects with such vast intelligence."[6]

In his notes on the state of Virginia, Thomas Jefferson, America's third president and the principal mind behind the Declaration of Independence, writes, "The first elements of morality too may be instilled into their [youths'] minds; such as, when further developed as their judgments advance in strength, may teach them how to work out their own greatest happiness [Phil. 2:12], by shewing them that it does not depend on the condition of life in which chance has placed them, but is always the result of a good conscience, good health, occupation, and freedom in all just pursuits."[7]

Jefferson references Philippians 2:12, which says, "Therefore, my dear friends, as you have always obeyed—not only in my presence, but now much more in my absence—continue to work out your salvation with fear and trembling."

Later, in a letter to his friend and rival John Adams (October 12, 1813), Jefferson writes of his affection for the Psalms: "Yet in the contemplation of a being so superlative [God], the hyperbolic flights of the Psalmist may often be followed with approbation, even with rapture; and I have no hesitation in giving him the psalm over all the Hymnists of every language, and of every time. Turn to the 148th psalm. . . . Have such conceptions been ever before expressed?"[8]

And we can't forget Benjamin Franklin, who knew the Bible well. Thomas Kidd, in his biography of Franklin, states that Franklin knew the Bible "backward and forward" and had read the Bible all the way through by age five![9] Franklin didn't just commit passages of the Bible to memory; it influenced the way he thought and even spoke.[10] Of the Bible, Franklin said, "A Bible and a newspaper in every house, a good school in every district—all studied and appreciated as they merit—are the principal support of virtue, morality and civil liberty."[11]

Other leaders and luminaries highly regarded the Bible and promoted reading it as well as learning from it. It is said that the great Victorian poet Alfred Lord Tennyson, appointed as England's poet laureate by Queen Victoria, said, "Bible reading is an education in itself."[12] The famous Civil War general Ulysses S. Grant was no saint.[13] The gruff West Point general and president didn't attend church because he didn't like the music. But he said, "The Bible is the anchor of our liberties."[14]

The German Romantic writer and poet Johann Wolfgang von

Goethe knew the practical power of the principles found in the Bible. He writes, "It is belief in the Bible, the fruits of deep meditation, which has served me as the guide of my moral and literary life. I have found capital safely invested and richly productive of interest, although I have sometimes made but a bad use of it."[15]

The esteemed Father of Enlightenment, Immanuel Kant, said, "The existence of the Bible, as a book for the people, is the greatest benefit which the human race has ever experienced. Every attempt to belittle it is a crime against humanity."

The noted English Victorian art critique John Ruskin was known to have committed long passages of Scripture to memory, thanks to the rigorous education he received from his mother. He writes, "Whatever merit there is in anything that I have written is simply due to the fact that when I was a child my mother daily read me a part of the Bible and daily made me learn a part of it by heart."[16]

Queen Elizabeth, the Queen Mother, noted, "Men turn this way and that in their search for new sources of comfort and inspiration, but the enduring truths are to be found in the Word of God."[17]

Maybe the former U.S. senator and secretary of state Edward Everett summed up the influence of the Bible upon society and the world best when he said, "The highest historical probability can be adduced in support of the proposition that, if it were possible to annihilate the Bible, and with it all its influences, we should destroy with it the whole spiritual system of the moral world—all our great moral ideas—refinement of manners—a constitutional government—equitable administration and security of property—our schools, hospitals, and benevolent associations—the press, the fine arts, the equality of the sexes, and the blessings of the fireside."[18]

The English Romantic poet Samuel Taylor Coleridge, admired as a poet as well as a theologian, expressed a similar sentiment about the Bible when he said, "For more than a thousand years the Bible, collectively taken, has gone hand in hand with civilization, science, law—in short, with the moral and intellectual cultivation of the species—always supporting, and often leading the way."[19]

It seems odd that in today's world, too often we neglect the wisdom of our forefathers. Times do change, but does time make irrelevant what many see as timeless truths, wise guidance, and society's indispensable foundation? C. S. Lewis called this way of thinking "chronological snobbery," which he described as calling old ways of thinking irrelevant simply because they are old.

No doubt, some people don't know what to do with some of the bold claims found in the Bible. We think those claims are worth considering.

# CHAPTER 18

# THE STORY THAT
# NEVER ENDS

*"Surely I am with you always, to the very end of the age."*
—MATTHEW 28:20

*Even the short history of Christianity in the region indicates how
the hopes of the powerful are subverted by the unexpected, for the
God of the Bible is full of Surprises.*
—IAN BREWARD, *INTRODUCTION TO
WORLD CHRISTIAN HISTORY*

*There is no "better place" than this, not in this world. And it is by
the place we've got, and our love for it and keeping of it, that this
world is joined to Heaven.*
—WENDELL BERRY, *HANNAH COULTER*

We began this book telling you our story, how we began collecting biblical artifacts, and what prompted us to keep at it. We've also told you about how the Bible has impacted our own family.

The star of this book, however, is and should be the Bible itself. The Bible tells a grand narrative of God's rescue mission for the world. From our point of view, it is a love story with a divine mission. You don't have to believe that, but our simple point is that the Bible stacks up pretty well against all other works of classical literature. For that reason, it deserves a fair hearing, and we should take seriously this grand narrative. Which means realizing we are all part of the story!

## A Story Unending

One of the spaces that I love in the museum is the temporary exhibit space. There is no building that can contain this book's story. Just about any exhibit we have could fill the museum. As an obvious example, we could look at art. The whole museum could be filled with biblical art many times over. The temporary exhibit space gives us the ability to do a deeper dive into any area of the Bible's story. That is similar to what John felt about the life of Jesus.

John concludes his gospel account by saying, "Jesus did many other things as well. If every one of them were written down, I suppose that even the whole world would not have room for the books that would be written" (John 21:25). Can you imagine? As if the miracles and wonderful orations weren't enough. Jesus did even more, so much more than we are aware of.

Can you see John, sitting there on the island of Patmos all these years later, writing down his account of the life of Jesus and smiling? He's smiling because as he's writing down the story of when Jesus raised Lazarus from the dead, another scene pops into his mind.

"Oh yeah, that would be so great to share. But I'm out of papyrus!"

Of course, we don't know if John really thought that. But he does allude to the fact that he carries many more memories with him. Maybe he's using a bit of hyperbole, but the point is, in the gospel accounts in the pages of our Bibles, we have only a snapshot of Jesus' life.

Think about all that's missing. The last thing we hear about his childhood is when he stayed behind in Jerusalem after the Passover festival while his parents walked on ahead, heading home. Mary and Joseph realized he wasn't in the caravan of people and had to walk all the way back into the city. After three days of searching for Jesus there, they finally found the twelve-year-old boy in the temple, "sitting among the teachers, listening to them and asking them questions" (Luke 2:46). This passage in Luke's gospel account ends like this: "Then he went down to Nazareth with them and was obedient to them. But his mother treasured all these things in her heart. And Jesus grew in wisdom and stature, and in favor with God and man" (vv. 51–52).

The next time we see Jesus, he's about thirty years old!

What happened during those eighteen years? This gap in Jesus' life invites speculation and some creative storytelling. But no one really knows. Just imagine the stories Jesus told his disciples of his life as they sat around the fire or walked the shoreline of the Sea of Galilee. Imagine how many more miracles were *not* recorded by the gospel accounts. Imagine the stories!

So there's John, sitting on his writing stone on the island of Patmos. He's finished his gospel account and now puts the finishing touches on what we know as the concluding book of the New Testament and the whole Bible. The book of Revelation.

John begins the book by saying, "The revelation from Jesus Christ, which God gave him to show his servants what must soon take place. He made it known by sending his angel to his servant John, who testifies to everything he saw—that is, the word of God and the testimony of Jesus Christ. Blessed is the one who reads aloud the words of this prophecy, and blessed are those who hear it and take to heart what is written in it, because the time is near" (Rev. 1:1–3).

What does he mean, the time is near? He means that the conclusion to this story of God pursuing the human race is close. And isn't it interesting that John includes a blessing here for the people who read this book out loud and take it seriously.

The book of Revelation receives plenty of skepticism from both opponents of religion and those who profess to believe what's in the book. Theologians don't know what to do with it. It's full of incredible imagery—the kind you'd find in a superhero movie.

John ends Revelation by saying, "I warn everyone who hears the words of the prophecy of this scroll: If anyone adds anything to them, God will add to that person the plagues described in this scroll. And if anyone takes words away from this scroll of prophecy, God will take away from that person any share in the tree of life and in the Holy City, which are described in this scroll" (Rev. 22:18–19).

Pretty hefty consequences for messing with this book of Scripture. But, in fact, John ends his book in a fashion similar to that of other writers of his day and before. Commentators tell us that John's final words here were customary in ancient times to protect what was written from future editors, mutilation, interpolations, and the like.

It's also interesting that John's book should actually be read as a letter. This makes the message personal. We are told to read Revelation with an eye toward personal application. We should also consider the concluding remarks that follow John's warning: "He who testifies to these things says, 'Yes, I am coming soon.' Amen. Come, Lord Jesus" (Rev. 22:20).

Here we find the cliff-hanger to the story! At the end of the Bible, Jesus says, "I am coming soon." That is to say, Jesus will return—or come again, as they say. In Matthew's gospel account, Jesus reminds his followers to "keep watch, because you do not know on what day your Lord will come" (Matt. 24:42). Talk about a tension builder!

John suggests that the response of the reader, who is most likely a believer of the message found throughout the Bible, is a hearty "Yes, Lord, come again. And do it soon!"

Can you sense the element of anticipation? The element of "To be continued"?

## A Supposal

The well-known children's book writer C. S. Lewis loved to use "supposals." Unlike a proposal, which proposes an idea, Lewis's supposals asked readers to consider a reality in which something was actually true. What he wanted readers to do was use their imaginations to suspend their disbelief.

So let's stop and suppose for a minute that the Bible is not true. Let's suppose it's just a book of fables.

That supposal leads to lots of questions.

What drove the writers in different ages to keep writing and to keep tying it back to one theme? It's hard enough to get five people together in a conference room and agree on a meeting agenda, let alone a book. Given all the writers, yet still the common theme, what made the book become so beloved that billions of people have sought it out as a source of truth? Why would different writers in different time periods continue pressing on with the same fable?

But let's keep supposing.

Let's suppose the idea of church discussed in the Bible is a myth. Consider the efforts of churches around the world. Think about the large cathedrals around the globe. Some huge. Some ornate. Some simple.

In our country alone, our Sundays are marked by millions of people who walk through the church doors to hear about a fable? Not only do they attend those churches, but they pay to be part of them.

They give to them.

They help them grow.

They give their cash to those churches even when they could spend it on themselves. Doesn't it seem crazy to give your money to a fable?

Let's suppose the Bible's call to teach this book is a lie.

What about the colleges, universities, and seminaries that each year charge people thousands of dollars to learn about the intricacies of this book? These places have trained professors—paid thinkers—who still write, theorize, and research about the teachings there. They debate them. They argue about theologies.

Of course, students graduate from these institutions and go out and plant churches or join established ones. All across the board, they write books to inspire, to give hope, and to go deeper into the teachings of the Bible. All throughout time, this has led to new institutions, new places of learning, that spring up to forward particular schools of thought.

Perhaps the Bible is merely words on a page. Maybe a good read, complicated at times, boring at others, but just a good read. Why are people still translating it, and not just into one language but into every known language in the world? The translation efforts are both written and oral. Shouldn't we be tired of the mere words on the page?

There's a more troubling supposal. Maybe the book doesn't contain any truth, any principles to live and die for. What then shall we say to the countless martyrs who have gone before—those who have bled and died excruciating deaths? Shall we say it is just an untruth? What about the missionaries who still to this day go to the crowded cities, the rural areas, and the remotest parts of the earth to proclaim its truth?

Shall we call them misguided?

Or perhaps unstable?

Let's go back to the ideas in chapter 15, and the impact of the Bible on the world. Let's suppose for a minute that the Bible had never been written. Let's question where Thomas Jefferson would have gone for a source document saying that the Creator endowed all people with inalienable rights of life, liberty, and the pursuit of happiness. And if there had been another source document, could it have endured with the longevity of the Bible?

Let's pause for a big supposal. If there had been no Bible, would there have been an American Revolution, a French Revolution, a Gandhi, a Nelson Mandela, a Martin Luther King Jr.?

How many revolutions might have died, and how long might oppression have survived but for the Bible?

What do we do with these supposals?

We have told you that we live our lives using the Bible as our guide. If it is not true, what should be our guide? If it is not true, then why should we care about one another? Why not buy the biggest yacht so we can go eat, drink, and be merry?

Why should anybody care about anybody else if all we have in this life is this life?

On the other hand, let's suppose that the Bible is true.

Actually, let's just make the supposal that the Bible *might* be true. Let's just suppose that it has enough historical evidence to make it worthy of consideration. Let's suppose that it has in fact made a difference in our world. If we make these kinds of supposals, then perhaps the Bible should be considered and taught.

To be clear, we are not saying and have never said that it must be believed. To the contrary, we are simply saying that this is a book that should be considered, read, and studied. The conclusions are for each individual reader to arrive at.

## This Dangerous Book

We never thought we'd be biblical artifact collectors. In reality, in this world, it would have been easier and far less costly not to be.

But we've grown up with the Bible, and we've seen it taught and lived out by others who have gone before us. Those examples gave us the courage to go on this adventure. As we took the step down this road, we've discovered a world far richer and far more beautiful than we could ever have imagined. We've grown deeper in our confidence about this book.

The story of the Bible is a big story, an enduring one, and one that transcends time and any one person or nation. We simply invite you to examine its narrative, its history, and its impact.

That's our invitation.

The response is yours to make. There's a bit of risk involved in that invitation. We believe there's also incredible reward.

Part of the dream of the museum was that we could see millions of people wandering the halls. They'd wander at a leisurely pace, with an honest, unbiased presentation. As they wandered those halls, they'd explore.

They'd question.

They'd look to their past.

They might question the future.

And they'd engage with this book, the Bible.

That's our supposal.

That's been our journey behind the museum. That's been the journey of our own lives. Suppose we could engage our world in a fresh set of conversations about beauty, bravery, the heart of man, and the place of God in the world.

We are dreamers enough to suppose, to think, that creating a place for the bestselling book of all time can promote meaningful conversations that produce understanding, change, and peace.

We may not all end up in the same place of belief. That's okay. But to not engage in the conversation and the journey seems to shutter ourselves from an entire narrative. Even the best-thinking minds would not agree with that supposal.

# NOTES

## Chapter 1: On a Plane to a Holy Grail

1. Janet Soskice, *The Sisters of Sinai: How Two Lady Adventurers Discovered the Hidden Gospels* (New York: Vintage, 2010), 80.
2. Ibid., 98.
3. Ibid., 3–6.
4. David Noel Freedman, *Eerdmans Dictionary of the Bible* (Grand Rapids: Eerdmans, 2000), 267.
5. Constantine Tischendorf, *Tischendorf on the Gospels*, Accordance electronic ed. (New York: American Tract Society, 1866), 27.

## Chapter 2: A Codex in a Cat Basket

1. *Letters of C. S. Lewis*, ed. W. H. Lewis (New York: Harcourt Brace Jovanovich, 1966), 247.
2. Oxford Bibliographies, www.oxfordbibliographies.com/view/document/obo-9780195396584/obo-9780195396584-0125.xml (accessed May 1, 2017).
3. Sotheby's, www.sothebys.com/en/auctions/ecatalogue/lot.48.html/2009/western-manuscripts-l09741 (accessed July 24, 2017).
4. Ibid.
5. Neil R. Lightfoot, *How We Got the Bible* (Grand Rapids: Baker, 2010), 22.
6. Ibid., 17.
7. Susan Adams, "1,500-Year-Old Hidden Record of Christ's Words," *Forbes* (June 26, 2009), *www.forbes.com/2009/06/26/ancient-bible-auction-lifestyle-collecting-bible-codex.html*. For more on the story behind CCR, see David Trobisch et al., *Verbum Domini II: God's Word Goes Out to the Nations* (Washington, D.C.: Museum of the Bible, 2014), 29.
8. Ibid., 23.

## Chapter 3: The Journey beyond Istanbul

1. Kenneth A. Briggs, *The Invisible Bestseller: Searching for the Bible in America* (Grand Rapids: Eerdmans, 2016), 5.
2. Alfred J. Hoerth, *Archaeology and the Old Testament* (Grand Rapids: Baker, 2009), 28.
3. "Leif Eriksson vs. Christopher Columbus," *History, www.history.com/topics/ exploration/exploration-of-north-america/videos/leif-eriksson-vs-christopher -columbus* (accessed May 31, 2017).

## Chapter 4: Book of Wonder: The Story of the Bible

1. Henry H. Halley, *Halley's Bible Handbook with the New International Version* (Grand Rapids: Zondervan, 2000).
2. Madeline L'Engle, "Newbery Award Acceptance Speech: The Expanding Universe" (August 1963), *www.madeleinelengle.com/wordpress/wp-content/ uploads/2011/08/Newbery_Award.pdf* (accessed May 4, 2017).
3. Halley, *Halley's Bible Handbook*, 24.
4. "History of the Wunderkammern (Cabinet of Curiosities)," *www.tate.org.uk/ learn/online-resources/mark-dion-tate-thames-dig/wunderkammen* (accessed April 24, 2017).
5. You can read the story of David and his adventures and mishaps in the books of 1 and 2 Samuel. This passage is taken from 1 Samuel 17 (MSG).

## Chapter 6: A Good Book

1. Rand Paul and James Randall Robison, *Our Presidents and Their Prayers: Proclamations of Faith by America's Leaders* (New York: Center Street, 2015), 11.
2. "Religious Quotations by Abraham Lincoln," *www.abrahamlincolnonline.org/ lincoln/speeches/faithquotes.htm* (accessed August 25, 2016).
3. Wayne A. Grudem, *Politics according to the Bible: A Comprehensive Resource for Understanding Modern Political Issues in Light of Scripture* (Grand Rapids: Zondervan, 2010), 262.
4. "What Is the Judeo-Christian Ethic?" *GotQuestions.org, www.gotquestions.org/ Judeo-Christian-ethic.html* (accessed August 25, 2016).

## Chapter 7: A Most Dangerous Book

1. J. H. Merle d'Aubigne, *The Reformation in England*, vol. 2 (Edinburgh: Banner of Truth, 1963), 48–52. Adapted for this publication.
2. Carole Jeanne Robarchek and Clayton Robarchek, *Waorani: The Contexts of Violence and War*, 1st ed. (Fort Worth, IN: Wadsworth, 1997), 198.
3. Ibid., 36.

## Chapter 8: The Museum of the Bible

1. Angelo Roncalli quoted in James Martin, *My Life with the Saints* (Chicago: Loyola, 2007), 210.
2. C. S. Lewis, *God in the Dock* (Grand Rapids: Eerdmans, 2014), 102.
3. Ariel Sabar, "Unearthing the World of Jesus," *Smithsonian.com, www.smithsonian mag.com/history/unearthing-world-jesus-180957515/* (accessed June 25, 2017).
4. Ibid.
5. "How the Romans Used Crucifixion—Including Jesus's—as a Political Weapon," *Newsweek* (April 4, 2015), *www.newsweek.com/how-romans-used -crucifixion-including-jesus-political-weapon-318934.*
6. Sabar, "Unearthing the World of Jesus."

## Chapter 9: The Dead Sea and the First Scriptures

1. "Paul's Use of Old Testament Scripture," Religious Studies Center, *https://rsc .byu.edu/archived/selected-articles/paul-s-use-old-testament-scripture* (accessed July 25, 2017).
2. Leland Ryken, Philip Ryken, and Jim Wilhoit, *Ryken's Bible Handbook* (Wheaton, IL: Tyndale, 2005), 631.
3. Randall Price, *Secrets of the Dead Sea Scrolls* (Eugene, OR: Harvest House, 1996), 35.
4. Ibid.
5. Ibid.
6. Ibid.
7. Ibid.
8. Ibid., 37.
9. Josh McDowell, *The New Evidence That Demands a Verdict*, revised and updated ed. (Nashville: Nelson, 1999), 90.
10. Ibid.

## Chapter 10: The New Scriptures

1. Walter Isaacson, *Einstein: His Life and Universe* (New York: Simon and Schuster, 2007), 386.
2. Craig S. Keener, *The IVP Bible Background Commentary: New Testament*, accordance electronic ed. (Downers Grove, IL: InterVarsity, 1993), 320.
3. Josh McDowell, *The New Evidence That Demands a Verdict*, revised updated ed. (Nashville: Nelson, 1999), 35.
4. The contemporary version of "One Solitary Life" is adapted and attributed to a sermon by Dr. James Allan Francis. For the edited text, see "Respectfully Quoted: A Dictionary of Quotations," Bartleby.com, *www.bartleby.com/73/ 916.html* (accessed July 25, 2017). For the original sermon, see James Allan Francis, *The Real Jesus and Other Sermons* (Judson, 1926). For biographical

details about James Allan Francis, see "One Solitary Life," *Celebrating Holidays*, *www.celebratingholidays.com/?page_id=4456* (accessed July 25, 2017).

5. "Josephus' Writings and Their Relation to the New Testament," *Bible.org*, *https://bible.org/article/josephus percentE2 percent80 percent99-writings-and -their-relation-new-testament* (accessed June 25, 2017).

6. McDowell, *New Evidence*, 121.

7. Michael J. Wilkins, *Jesus Under Fire: Modern Scholarship Reinvents the Historical Jesus* (Grand Rapids, MI: Zondervan, 1996), 221–22.

## Chapter 11: A Special Book

1. Martin H. Manser, *The Westminster Collection of Christian Quotations* (Louisville: Westminster John Knox, 2001), 264.

2. Ibid., 22.

## Chapter 12: Revolution: The Bible and America

1. Rand Paul and James Randall Robison, *Our Presidents and Their Prayers: Proclamations of Faith by America's Leaders* (New York: Center Street, 2015), 132.

2. This phrase was used by the revolutionaries, but it came from John Locke's treatise *Two Treatises of Government*. Here's the passage, which refers not only to an appeal for human justice but also to an appeal to heaven by anyone who suffers unjust treatment: "What is my Remedy against a Robber, that so broke into my House? Appeal to the Law for Justice. But perhaps Justice is denied, or I am crippled and cannot stir, robbed and have not the means to do it. If God has taken away all means of seeking remedy, there is nothing left but patience. But my Son, when able, may seek the Relief of the Law, which I am denied: He or his Son may renew his Appeal, till he recovers his Right. But the Conquered, or their Children, have no Court, no Arbitrator on Earth to appeal to. Then they may appeal, as Jephtha did, to Heaven, and repeat their Appeal, till they have recovered the native Right of their Ancestors, which was to have such a Legislative over them, as the Majority should approve, and freely acquiesce in."

3. Thomas S. Kidd, *God of Liberty: A Religious History of the American Revolution* (New York: Basic, 2012), 6–10.

4. Ibid., 7.

5. William J. Bennett, *The Moral Compass: Stories for a Life's Journey* (New York: Simon and Schuster, 1995), 593.

6. George Washington, "On Braddock's Defeat," Annals of American History. You can read the letter in its original handwriting at the Library of Congress: "George Washington Papers at the Library of Congress, 1741–1799: Series 2 Letterbooks," *http://memory.loc.gov/cgi-bin/ampage?collId=mgw2&fileName =gwpage001.db&recNum=84&tempFile=./temp/percent7Eammem_kmEd&file*

*code=mgw&next_filecode=mgw&itemnum=1&ndocs=1241read percent20*
(accessed July 25, 2017).

## Chapter 13: Revolutionary: A Nation of the Book

1. Daniel L. Dreisbach, *Reading the Bible with the Founding Fathers* (Oxford, UK; New York: Oxford Univ. Press, 2016), 1.
2. John Cotton, ed., *The New-England Primer: Improved for the More Easy Attaining the True Reading of English: To Which Is Added The Assembly of Divines, and Mr. Cotton's Catechism* (Aledo, TX: WallBuilder Press, 1991), foreword.
3. Ibid., "The Shorter Catechism."
4. Daniel L. Dreisbach, *Reading the Bible with the Founding Fathers* (Oxford, UK; New York: Oxford Univ. Press, 2016), 37.
5. Ibid.
6. Rob Cooper, "Forcing a Religion on Your Children Is as Bad as Child Abuse, Claims Atheist Professor Richard Dawkins," *DailyMail.com* (April 22, 2013), *www.dailymail.co.uk/news/article-2312813/Richard-Dawkins-Forcing-religion -children-child-abuse-claims-atheist-professor.html*.
7. Richard Dawkins, "Why I Want All Our Children to Read the King James Bible," *The Guardian*, May 19, 2012, sec. Opinion, *http://www.theguardian .com/science/2012/may/19/richard-dawkins-king-james-bible*.
8. "The Bible's Influence: The Bible as Cultural Influence," *Washington Times*, *www.washingtontimes.com/news/2014/dec/11/the-bibles-influence-the-bible-as -cultural-influen/* (accessed May 25, 2017).
9. "The Bible's Influence: The Bible and Public Schools, a First Amendment Guide," *Washington Times*, *www.washingtontimes.com/news/2014/dec/11/the -bibles-influence-the-bible-public-schools-a-fi/* (accessed May 25, 2017).
10. Martin H. Manser, *The Westminster Collection of Christian Quotations* (Louisville: Westminster John Knox , 2001), 22.
11. Anne Rice, "Appendice," in *Christ the Lord: Out of Egypt* (New York: Ballantine, 2008), 331–32.
12. Benjamin Rush, *A Defence of the Use of the Bible in Schools* (American Tract Society, 1820).

## Chapter 14: The Adventure of the Bible

1. David Trobisch et al., *Verbum Domini II: God's Word Goes out to the Nations* (Washington, DC: Museum of the Bible, 2014), 101–4.
2. Ibid., 168–69.

## Chapter 15: Godly Architecture: How the Bible Shaped Our World

1. Vishal Mangalwadi, *The Book That Made Your World: How the Bible Created the Soul of Western Civilization* (Nashville: Nelson, 2011), 2.

2. Douglas Brinkley, *Time: The 100 Most Influential People of All Time* (New York: Time, 2012), 37.

3. Kelly Knauer et al., *History's Greatest Events: 100 Turning Points That Changed the World: An Illustrated Journey* (New York: Time, 2010).

4. Ibid., 9.

5. Ibid., 21.

6. Ibid., 22.

7. Ibid., 45.

8. Ibid., 51.

9. Ibid., 55.

10. Ibid.

11. "Nicholas Copernicus: Revolutionary Astronomer," *Christianity Today*, www.christianitytoday.com/history/people/scholarsandscientists/nicholas-copernicus.html (accessed July 27, 2017).

12. Knauer et al., *History's Greatest Events*, 57.

13. Ibid., 58.

14. "The Faith behind the Famous: Isaac Newton," *Christianity Today*, www.christianitytoday.com/history/issues/issue-30/faith-behind-famous-isaac-newton.html (accessed July 27, 2017).

15. Ibid.

16. Knauer et al., *History's Greatest Events*, 68.

17. Ibid., 90.

18. "A Thank-You Note from the *Amistad* Rebels to One of Their Lawyers, John Quincy Adams," *Slate* (July 7, 2014), www.slate.com/blogs/the_vault/2014/07/07/amistad_john_quincy_adams_history_thank_you_note_from_the_rebels_to_one.html.

19. John Quincy Adams, argument before the Supreme Court in the *Amistad* case (1841).

20. Jonathan Bean, ed., *Race and Liberty in America: The Essential Reader* (Lexington: The Univ. Press of Kentucky, 2009), 29–30.

21. Ibid., 30.

22. John Quincy Adams, *Letters of John Quincy Adams to His Son on the Bible and Its Teachings* (New York: Derby, Miller, and Co., 1850), 9–10.

## Chapter 16: The Opposition

1. "Fox's Book of Martyrs," www.ccel.org/f/foxe/martyrs/home.html (accessed May 23, 2017). Today you can purchase *Foxe's Book of Martyrs* or access it from your smartphone or computer. If you're interested in discovering more about the hardships of the early Christians, visit this website for a brief sketch of John Foxe himself, and the entire text of his book for free.

2. "Fox's Book of Martyrs," *www.biblestudytools.com/history/foxs-book-of-martyrs/* (accessed May 23, 2017).

3. Morgan Lee, "Sorry, Tertullian," *ChristianityToday, www.christianitytoday.com/ct/2014/december/sorry-tertullian.html* (accessed May 23, 2017).

4. Kenneth Scott Latourette, *A History of Christianity: Beginnings to 1500* (Peabody, MA: Prince Press, 1997), 92.

5. Ibid.

6. Randall Price, *Searching for the Original Bible* (Eugene, OR: Harvest House, 2007), 52, 157.

7. See Lautaurette, highlighted chapter on the spread of Christianity.

8. Derek Cooper, *Introduction to World Christian History* (Downers Grove, IL: InterVarsity, 2016), 79.

9. Ibid.

10. Ibid., 147.

11. "The Bible Translation That Rocked the World," *Christianity Today, christianitytoday.com/history/issues/issue-34/bible-translation-that-rocked-world.html* (accessed May 24, 2017).

12. Ibid., 148.

13. Martin H. Manser, *The Westminster Collection of Christian Quotations* (Louisville: Westminster John Knox, 2001), 24.

14. Paul Marshall, Lela Gilbert, and Nina Shea, *Persecuted: The Global Assault on Christians* (Nashville: Nelson, 2013), 264.

15. Ibid., 1.

16. Ibid., 175.

17. Timothy Beal, *The Rise and Fall of the Bible: The Unexpected History of an Accidental Book* (Boston: Mariner, 2012), 171.

18. Bertrand Russell, *Why I Am Not a Christian and Other Essays on Religion and Related Subjects*, ed. Paul Edwards (New York: Touchstone, 1967), 22.

19. Christopher Hitchens, *God Is Not Great: How Religion Poisons Everything* (New York: Twelve, 2009), 102.

## Chapter 17: What Has Been Said about This Amazing Book

1. "TV Ratings: History's 'The Bible' Pulls 11.7 Million Viewers with Easter Ender," *Hollywood Reporter, www.hollywoodreporter.com/live-feed/tv-ratings-historys-bible-pulls-432045* (accessed June 26, 2017).

2. "What Do Americans Really Think about the Bible?" Barna Group, *www.barna.com/research/what-do-americans-really-think-about-the-bible/* (accessed June 26, 2017).

3. Martin H. Manser, *The Westminster Collection of Christian Quotations* (Louisville: Westminster John Knox , 2001), 21.

4. St. Augustine, *Saint Augustine Confessions* (Oxford: Oxford Univ. Press, 1998), 40.

5. Abraham Lincoln, *The Collected Works of Abraham Lincoln*, vol. 2, ed. Roy Basler, History Book Club ed. (Rutgers Univ. Press, 1953), 542.

6. Charles W. Eliot, ed., *Prefaces and Prologues to Famous Books*, The Harvard Classics, vol. 39 (New York: Collier and Son, 1965), 386.

7. Thomas Jefferson, *Jefferson: Writings*, ed. Merrill D. Peterson (New York: Library of America, 1984), 273.

8. Lester J. Cappon, ed., *The Adams-Jefferson Letters: The Complete Correspondence between Thomas Jefferson and Abigail and John Adams* (Chapel Hill, NC: Univ. of North Carolina Press, 1988), 385.

9. Thomas S. Kidd, *Benjamin Franklin: The Religious Life of a Founding Father* (New Haven, CT: Yale Univ. Press, 2017), 5, 18.

10. Ibid.

11. Upper Room Bible Class, *Upper Room Bulletin* (Ann Arbor, MI: 1917), 69.

12. Roy B. Zuck, *The Speaker's Quote Book: Over 5,000 Illustrations and Quotations for All Occasions*, revised and expanded ed. (Grand Rapids: Kregel, 2009), 38.

13. "What About Ulysses S. Grant?" *Christianity Today*, www.christianitytoday.com/history/issues/issue-33/what-about-ulysses-s-grant.html (accessed June 26, 2017).

14. Zuck, *Speaker's Quote Book*, 38.

15. Ibid., 30.

16. Ibid.

17. Ibid., 402.

18. Samuel Austin Allibone, *The Union Bible Companion; Containing the Evidences of the Divine Origin . . . of the Holy Scriptures. An Account of Various Manuscripts, and English Translations, Etc* (American Sunday-School Union, 1871), 156.

19. Ibid., 155.

# PHOTO CREDITS

# INDEX